YIELDED BODIES

YIELDED BODIES

by
ROBERT G. LEE, D.D.
Pastor, Bellvue Baptist Church,
Memphis, Tennessee

ZONDERVAN PUBLISHING HOUSE
Grand Rapids, Michigan

I beseech you therefore, brethren, by the mercies of God, that ye present your bodies a living sacrifice, holy, acceptable unto God, which is your reasonable service.
Romans 12:1

CONTENTS

Chapter One

THE HUMAN BODY

I will praise thee; for I am fearfully and wonderfully made: marvellous are thy works; and that my soul knoweth right well (Ps. 139:14).

Know ye not that ye are the temple of God, and that the Spirit of God dwelleth in you? (I Cor. 3:16)

We live in a world of wonder, wonders and wondering. Said James Gates Percival:

> The world is full of poetry — the air
> Is living with its spirit; and the waves
> Dance to the music of its melody.

And Shakespeare exclaimed:

> O wonderful, wonderful, and most
> Wonderful, wonderful.

Thus we feel when we think of the marvels, the wonders, of this universe and the marvels of the animal kingdom, the mineral kingdom, the vegetable kingdom, the bird world, and the astronomical realms.

Think of the marvels of the mechanical world that almost awake in us a primeval faith in magic, marvels which annihilate distance, make ice in the tropics, grow oranges in the snow, make a messenger boy out of the lightning, marvels which make art to rejoice and science to exult.

Think of the jet planes which mount up with such speed as to be almost as fast as the lightning that flashes out of the far west unto the distant east.

Think of the great reapers, "careening like yachts through seas of waving wheat," that have taken the place of the old

7

scythe which the Egyptians used on the banks of the Nile or the Babylonians in the Euphrates valley.

Think of the scientific marvel of compressing a Caruso into the microscopic point of a needle and imprisoning Sousa's brass band in a wax disc.

Think of the chemical marvel of putting seven-tenths of one per cent chromium into low carbon steel and increasing the tensile strength of that steel from 55,000 pounds to the square inch to 100,000 pounds to the square inch.

Think of the marvel in "the bird world" — such as the humming bird making two hundred strokes a second, as man found out by matching the bird's hum with a note on a violin. What a clever flier the humming bird is, with ability to rise straight up in perpendiculer speed in the air, to hover motionless before a flower, and to fly backwards as well as forwards. Think of the marvel, too, of the homing pigeon, which nurses in its strange little breast, for years, that directing sense of its way home, makes flight, as did Nansen's pigeon, over thousands of unmarked miles across an ocean and mountain wilderness, flies an unseen line and comes at last to the one window ledge in all the world where it was looked for.

Think of the marvels of the bee with wings which in flight beat 11,400 times a minute, which move in a figure-of-eight design, and which thus make flight in any direction possible — up, down, side to side, backward and forward.

Think of the marvel of honey making when we know that it takes about 37,000 loads of nectar to make one pound of honey and that the bees from one hive (say about 45,000) will visit more than 250,000 blossoms in one day to gather this amount, making a flight mileage of at least 50,000 miles.

Think of the marvels of instinct, or that sense of direction, or whatever you may term it, of the dog. This is shown by what W. H. Gambrell wrote to the *Boston Post* from Cambridge, Mass., about his dog, Vixen. Here it is:

"About two months ago when I came from my home in

Greenville, S. C., to Cambridge, I brought with me a very highly prized St. Bernard dog named Vixen, as I was very fond of him. I exercised great care that he should not get loose until he had become familiar with his new surroundings; but one bright morning some ten days after arriving here with him, I decided to let him have a sun bath by tying him in front of the house while I went to the postoffice for the mail. When I returned to the house thirty minutes later, to my great surprise, I found that Vixen had gnawed the leash in two and departed. I advertised for him in the papers, offering a liberal reward for his recovery, but all to no avail. I never heard anything from him. Yesterday I received a letter from home stating that Vixen had just arrived there in apparently good health. How a dog could find his way from here to Greenville, S.C. is more than I can understand."

Think of the astronomical wonders.

> The heavens declare the glory of God; and the firmament sheweth his handywork. Day unto day uttereth speech, and night unto night sheweth knowledge. There is no speech nor language, where their voice is not heard. Their line is gone out through all the earth, and their words to the end of the world. In them hath he set a tabernacle for the sun, which is as a bridegroom coming out of his chamber, and rejoiceth as a strong man to run a race. His going forth is from the end of the heaven, and his circuit unto the ends of it: and there is nothing hid from the heat thereof (Ps. 19:1-6).

Think of the architectural wonders of the Taj Mahal of Shah Jehan. Standing on the banks of the Jumna River at Agra, India, is the Taj Mahal, the love-tribute of Shah Jehan to Princess Arjamand, his wife, whom he called Mumtaz Mahal, the "exalted of the Palace," loved as few women have ever been loved. It is the most beautiful structure in the world. It is a dream in marble. It is, as some one has called it, "frozen poetry." "On each visit to Agra I have gone time and time again, at sunrise, at noon, and at sunset, and lingered for hours, now on the entrance gateway, now on the marble

approach, or again lying on the green sward, to gaze upon and
to drink in its wonderful beauty."

But think of the
MARVELS OF OUR MAKER'S MASTERPIECE

Greater than any temple built by man is the human body —
the greatest temple known to men.

Wonderful the framework, with two hundred bones in the
framework, not counting the bones in the ears; more durable
than steel, with every joint tightly enclosed, moving in a constant bath of oil and producing its own oil.

Wonderful the body's running gear — the muscles — with
its system of co-ordinate contractions among different groups of
muscles.

Wonderful the breather system of the human machine,
starting at the nose, with the thermostatic control — the lungs
and skin. Throughout every portion of the skin are found
millions of tiny glands.

A most marvelous fact about the human body is that its
life is not a single thing. It is made up of an immense number
of individual units, microscopic in size, each having a structure
of its own, a function of its own, a life of its own. So small
are they and so numerous that in a drop of blood as large as
a small pinhead, there are five million of them.

Can you imagine any human architect sitting down at a
desk and making declaration that he can plan a human body?
Is it not true, as one has stated, that the most eminent group
of anatomists and physiologists and scientists from every realm
could not, though they united their mentalities, though they
labored one thousand years, conceive or devise the thousands
of contrivances which confront us whenever and wherever
we touch the human body? Are not the leading scientists
baffled and profoundly conscious of the impenetrable mystery
which encircles them as they study the human body?

Is the efficiency of any modern machine about which

engineers talk as great as the efficiency of man's body when it functions in health and strength?

Is any pump as perfect as the human heart which, when properly cared for, stays on the job, though sometimes overworked, though sometimes poisoned, though sometimes overloaded, though sometimes thrown into high speed without going through the low gears, though abused in so many ways? Is it not wonderful the way it stays on the job, miraculously efficient in spite of the punishment it takes, making 4,320 strokes and pumping 15 gallons of blood an hour? In one year the heart beats 40,000,000 times, with no rest except between contractions. In the heart are 100,000 miles of blood vessels — a vast system through which the blood flows regularly.

Is any telegraphic mechanism equal to our nervous system? Is any radio so wonderful and so efficient as the voice and the ear? Is any camera as perfect as the human eye? Is any ventilating plant as wonderful as the nose, lungs and skin? The answer is *no*. Can any electrical switchboard compare with the brain? Is any cable as worthy of wonder as the spinal cord? Is not such a marvelous mechanism worthy of the highest respect and the best care? Yes! Is not the temple of the body to be kept clean? Yes!

All of which brings us to say that God made the human body — and it is his *masterpiece*.

> For the body is not one member, but many. If the foot shall say, Because I am not the hand, I am not of the body; is it therefore not of the body? And if the ear shall say, Because I am not the eye, I am not of the body; is it therefore not of the body? If the whole body were an eye, where were the hearing? If the whole were hearing, where were the smelling? But now hath God set the members every one of them in the body, as it hath pleased him. And if they were all one member, where were the body? But now are they many members, yet but one body. And the eye can not say unto the hand, I have no need of thee: nor again the head to the feet, I have no need of you. Nay, much more those members of the body, which seem to be more feeble, are necessary: and those members of the

> body, which we think to be less honourable, upon these we
> bestow more abundant honour; and our uncomely parts have
> more abundant comeliness. For our comely parts have no need:
> but God hath tempered the body together, having given more
> abundant honour to that part which lacked: that there should
> be no schism in the body; but that the members should have
> the same care one of another. And whether one member suffer,
> all the members suffer with it; or one member be honoured,
> all the members rejoice with it (I Cor. 12:14-26).

God's masterpiece — the human body — is the most exquisite and wonderful organization that has come from the
divine hand.

Now think of the
MASTERY OF THIS BODY

This mastery God urges:

> Let not sin therefore reign in your mortal body, that ye should
> obey it in the lusts thereof. Neither yield ye your members as
> instruments of unrighteousness unto sin: but yield yourselves
> unto God, as those that are alive from the dead, and your
> members as instruments of righteousness unto God. For sin shall
> not have dominion over you: for ye are not under the law, but
> under grace (Rom. 6:12-14).

This mastery Paul urged by word and by example:

> But I keep under my body, and bring it into subjection: lest
> that by any means, when I have preached to others, I myself
> should be a castaway (I Cor. 9:27).

This mastery is necessary because of the deadly doing of
sin in the body.

The destruction of sin is extensive. Sin abuses the body
and makes that which should be the temple of the Holy Ghost,
the temple which the Devil uses. As the traders in the Temple
at Jerusalem made God's house "a den of thieves," so sin
makes the human body a den where iniquities find dwelling
place and iniquities issue. As sin would pull God out of His
throne, abusing His authority, His justice, His power, His
wisdom, His patience, His mercy, His holiness, His promises,
so sin would abuse all the powers and defile all the precincts of
the human body.

There are many steps to Satan's ladder in this matter of his effort to devour the strength and mar the usefulness of the human body in which man should glorify God. A man comes first to walk in the counsel of the ungodly, then he stands in the way of sinners, and lastly sits in the seat of the scornful. Satan leads up the steps of his ladder. After temptation is offered, then comes approbation in the understanding. After that, consent in the will. After that comes practice in the affection. After that, custom in the repeated act. After that, delight in the sinful way. After that comes the defense of it, with all the rhetoric hell can invent. After that comes boldness in sinning. And last of all comes scorning and a drawing of "iniquity with cords of vanity" (Isa. 5:8), boasting in wickedness and glorying in shame. Satan acts like a creeping dragon and then like a flying serpent. His first request seems mannerly and modest, as Semiramis desired of Ninus to reign but one day, and that day to do what she pleased — and in that day she cut off his head. That is sin! Sin deceives man till man is hardened through its deceitfulness. It appears at first but little in the fountain, in the heart and thought. Then it bubbles into a stream of evil words; then it increases into a river of evil actions. Next it swells into a torrent and overflows till it drowns men in perdition. Thus it gradually destroys them.

Satan would have us forget these words:

> Meats for the belly, and the belly for meats: but God shall destroy both it and them. Now the body is not for fornication, but for the Lord; and the Lord for the body (I Cor. 6:13).

Satan would have our ears be deaf to the words:

> Ye are bought with a price: therefore glorify God in your body (I Cor. 6:20).

Mrs. Wilcox describes the deadly and dastardly doings of sin in the body in her poem which she calls "The Squanderer":

> God gave him passions splendid as the sun
> Meant for the lordliest purposes — a part
> Of Nature's full and fertile mother's heart,

From which new systems and new worlds are spun.
And now behold! Behold what he has done!
In Folly's court and Carnal Pleasure's mart
He flung the wealth God gave him at the start.
At dawn he stood potential, opulent,
With virile manhood and emotions keen.
At noon he stands — all Love's large fortune spent
In petty traffic, unproductive, mean —
A pauper cursed with impotent desire!

Stephen Phillips wrote:

Who stabs at this my heart stabs at a kingdom;
These veins are rivers, and these arteries
Are very roads; this body is your country.

But Carlyle showed how sin can stab and ruin the kingdom
of the body when he wrote:

Seated within this body's car,
The silent self is driven far,
And the five senses at the poles,
Like steeds are tugging restive of control.

And if the driver lose his way
Or the reins break, who can say
Into what blind paths, what pits of fear
Will plunge the chargers in their mad career?

The consoling fact that we *can* glorify God in the body urges
us that we should not let sin reign in our mortal bodies.
Our bodies are but dust, but they can bring praise to Him
who created the human body and set the members in place
as it pleased Him. Dull and tuneless in themselves — mere
houses of clay which we lease for just a few summers and
winters — they can be glorious harps on which the music
of piety can be struck to heaven. Though often assaulted by
disease, they can be channels through which the Divine shall
become articulate. No matter what temptations assail or what
difficulties surround us, we can glorify God in our mortal
bodies — if we will to, if we will. Paul taught that in these
words:

We are troubled on every side, yet not distressed; we are
perplexed, but not in despair; persecuted, but not forsaken; cast

down, but not destroyed; always bearing about in the body the
dying of the Lord Jesus, that the life also of Jesus might be
made manifest in our body. For we which live are alway
delivered unto death for Jesus' sake, that the life also of Jesus
might be made manifest in our mortal flesh (II Cor. 4:8-11).

And by presenting our bodies to God "as those who are alive
from the dead" and the members of our bodies as instruments
of righteousness unto God by always bearing in the body the
death of Jesus and manifesting the life of Jesus, we shall be
saved from reaping to the flesh.

Now the works of the flesh are manifest, which are these;
Adultery, fornication, uncleanness, lasciviousness, idolatry, witch-
craft, hatred, variance, emulations, wrath, strife, seditions, here-
sies, envyings, murders, drunkenness, revellings, and such like:
of the which I tell you before, as I have also told you in time
past, that they which do such things shall not inherit the kingdom of God (Gal. 5:19-21).

And the truth is that "he that soweth to his flesh shall of
the flesh reap corruption" (Gal. 6:8). Now, remember that
the body is not for fornication but for the Master.

Let us not forget that the body is

MORTAL

"Your mortal body," God says. And, if Jesus tarry in His
coming, the body shall wrestle with death. Death will close
the mortal eyes so that they shall see no more. Death will
deaden the ears so that they can hear never a voice or sound.
Death will stop the feet so that never a step will they take
again. Death will fold the hands so that no task they can do —
with pen or tool or touch. Death will silence the tongue so
that no word will be spoken. Death will still the heart so that
neither hate nor love shall abide there. "It is appointed unto
man once to *die*." "Your mortal body"!

What David once said to Jonathan we can say to others —
some younger and some older than are we: "Truly as the Lord
liveth, and as they soul liveth, there is but a step between
me and death" (I Sam. 20:3).

How grim a fact is death! The blackest shadow that ever wrapped this earth in darkness, it seems to blot out the lamps of life, of love, of hope, leaving people in ashes and grief, even in despair. Death, the one sanctity all men respect, the one gesture that melts the hardest, the one awe that appalls the most impious, the one great democrat, the one mocker at our aristocracies and high mightiness, the one commander whose words all obey, the one stroke of common sense that annihilates all our follies — death is also the one preacher of righteousness and truth and justice that gets the ears of all.

That step between us and death all must take — if Jesus tarry. The athlete must. The cripple must. The strong, the weak, the sick must. The rich must. The poor must. The black man must. The white man must! The scholar must. The ignoramus must. The king must. The beggar must. The millionaire must. The maiden must. All folks must.

Settle us in the finest spot under the fairest skies, beside the clearest streams, watching the choicest flowers, listening to the sweetest songs, yet even there that step would be before us and death find us. We can not escape taking it. We can not refuse to take it. We can not ask to be let off. We must follow in the train of all who have gone before us. "Death has passed upon all men." It is the one event that happeneth to all.

Remembering that your body is a mortal body, do not take the step between you and death without God. Do not take that step alone; alone without the Christ who can brighten or dispel every shadow; alone without Him who knows the way out of every difficulty; alone without Him who gave His body on the Cross for our sins, who lay in our grave and came forth that we might sit on His throne.

Let not sin reign in your body — lest you utter some remorseful wail akin to that uttered by Edward in *King Lear*:

> I have served the lust of my mistress heart and did the act of
> darkness with her. Swore as many oaths as I spake words and

broke them in the sweet face of heaven. . . . Wine loved I deeply, dice dearly, and in woman out-paramoured the Turk. False of heart, light of ear, bloody of hand. Hog in sloth, fox in stealth, wolf in greediness, dog in madness, lion in prey.

Yield your body to God.

> I beseech you therefore, brethren, by the mercies of God, that ye present your bodies a living sacrifice, holy, acceptable unto God, which is your reasonable service (Rom. 12:1).

And yield that body, so fearfully and wonderfully made, now. Be done with excuses. Be done with alibis.

Remember that Jesus looked upon His body as a temple.

> Jesus answered and said unto them, Destroy this temple, and in three days I will raise it up. Then said the Jews, Forty and six years was this temple in building, and wilt thou rear it up in three days? But he spake of the temple of his body (John 2: 19-21).

Remember that the bodies of Christians are the "members of Christ" (I Cor. 6:15) — and are the body of Christ (I Cor. 12:27).

Give ears keenly sensitized and wills obedient to the words of Paul who, by the Holy Spirit, wrote:

> Christ shall be magnified in my body (Phil. 1:20).

> What? know ye not that your body is the temple of the Holy Ghost which is in you, which ye have of God, and ye are not your own? For ye are bought with a price: therefore glorify God in your body, and in your spirit, which are God's (I Cor. 6:19-20).

Say with David:

> I will praise thee; for I am fearfully and wonderfully made: marvellous are thy works; and that my soul knoweth right well (Ps. 139:14).

See to it that you are always bearing about in the body the dying of the Lord Jesus so that the life also of Jesus might be made manifest in your body (II Cor. 4:10).

Then you will surely glorify God in your body and God will be glorified in your life as the sun is glorified in beautiful and fragrant flowers.

Chapter Two

THE EYES OF THE HUMAN BODY

*The light of the body is the eye: if therefore thine eye
be single, thy whole body shall be full of light. But if
thine eye be evil, thy whole body shall be full of darkness.
If therefore the light that is in thee be darkness, how
great is that darkness* (Matt. 6:22-23).
He that formed the eye, shall he not see? (Ps. 94:9).

With all his mechanical skill, man has never yet built a
machine that even approximates the precision, delicacy,
intricacy, mystery and durability of the human body.

With all the careful explorations and startling discoveries of
the physiologists, the wonderful story of the human body — the
body, "not for fornication but for the Lord," — has not been
told by half. Some of the processes of the human body are
so intricate that even today, after hundreds of years of painstaking investigation, they remain a complete mystery.

Who ever found, or can now find, any palace or cathedral
that held or holds, such severe beauty, such chaste proportions,
such marvelously wrought walls, such magnificent adornments
as are found in the human body?

Have you not read the romance of modern times as recited
in the discoveries in the human body — Harvey, with his
circulation of blood? Aselli, showing the existence of the
limphatic system of vessels? Hales, revealing the method of
the direct measurement of the blood pressure? Haller, with
his patient work on the muscles? Lavoisier, discovering oxygen
and showing its functions in respiration? And are not these

men but a few of the modern explorers of the human temple who stand before its countless mystic doors and add fresh emphasis to the Psalmist's words:

> For thou hast possessed my reins: thou hast covered me in my mother's womb. I will praise thee; for I am fearfully and wonderfully made: marvellous are thy works; and that my soul knoweth right well. My substance was not hid from thee, when I was made in secret, and curiously wrought in the lowest parts of the earth. Thine eyes did see my substance, yet being unperfect; and in thy book all my members were written, which in continuance were fashioned, when as yet there was none of them (Ps. 139:13-16).

Here is evidence of God's planning from the very moment of conception. God's signature, as in the book of nature, is written everywhere in the human body, showing us that a thing of such precision and accuracy could not have possibly come by chance or by evolution. Forget never that only God could conceive and create such a marvelous thing as the human body.

We must remember as we think of the body that "the body is more than raiment" (Luke 12:23); that "if ye live after the flesh, ye shall die: but if ye through the Spirit do mortify the deeds of the body, ye shall live" (Rom. 8:13); that we are to glorify God in the body (I Cor. 6:20) because "the body is not for fornication, but for the Lord; and the Lord for the body" (I Cor. 6:13). We, as believers, can never be found "always bearing about in the body the dying of the Lord Jesus, that the life also of Jesus might be made manifest in our body" (II Cor. 4:10), unless we give heed to these words:

> Know ye not that your bodies are the members of Christ? shall I then take the members of Christ, and make them the members of an harlot? God forbid. What? know ye not that he which is joined to an harlot is one body? for two, saith he, shall be one flesh. But he that is joined unto the Lord is one spirit. Flee fornication. Every sin that a man doeth is without the body; but he that committeth fornication sinneth against his own body (I Cor. 6:15-18).

In *Othello,* Iago says:

> Our bodies are gardens; to the which our wills are gardeners:
> so that if we will plant nettles or sow lettuce, set hyssop and
> weed up thyme, supply it with one gender of herbs or distract
> it with many, either to have it sterile with idleness or manured
> with industry, why, the power and corrigible authority of this
> lies in our wills. If the balance of our lives had not one scale of
> reason to poise another of sensuality, the blood and baseness of
> our natures would conduct us to more preposterous conclusions:
> but we have reason to cool our raging motions, our carnal
> stings, our unbitted lusts.

It is good for us to remember Shakespeare's words as we
hearken to Paul who said: "I keep under my body, and bring
it into subjection" (I Cor. 9:27).

Paul, urging upon us the wisdom of yielding our bodies to
God, speaks of "your members" — meaning the members of
our bodies. We have but to lose one of these members — a
hand or a finger on the hand, a foot or a toe on the foot, an
arm, a leg, an eye, a tooth, a part of the lip — to know the
value of every member of the body.

Our message today is one about the eyes. Consider the

MARVEL OF THE HUMAN EYE

The eye is the imperial organ of the human system. The
eye is mentioned 534 times in the Bible. In the Bible, God
honors the eye, extols the eye, illustrates the eye, arraigns the
eye, condemns the eye. And surgeons speak of the glories
of the eyes. And physiologists write much of the wonders of
the eyes. God is a God of infinite wisdom. Proof of this
is that He created the human eye. Had He been less than
infinite in wisdom, He could not have created the human eye.
"The hearing ear, and the seeing eye, the Lord hath made
even both of them" (Prov. 20:12).

God sings an anthem of praise to His own infinite wisdom
and creative power in human eyes. For there are eight
hundred contrivances in the human eye. Modern optometry

has developed a twenty-one point eye examination. There are twenty-one different measurements of the eye and its muscles. Of all the senses, sight is supreme. Although it is small as compared with some of the other faculties, the eye, by reason of the quality, the delicacy, the painstaking thought which has gone into its construction, reigns with a kind of undisputed kingship over all man's bodily powers.

It is wonderful how the eye can flash with indignation, kindle with enthusiasm, expand with devotion, melt with sympathy, stare with fright, leer with villiany, droop with sadness, pale with envy, fire with revenge, twinkle with mirth, beam with love, frown with wrath, contract with pain. The wise philosopher said: "An eye can threaten like a loaded and leveled gun, or can insult like hissing or kicking. In its altered moods, by beams of kindness, it can make the heart dance with joy." What a genius among the members of the human body is the eye!

Dr. Talmadge once said: "The eyes of Archibald Alexander and Charles S. Finney were the mightiest part of their sermons. The fire of spiritually passionate souls burned in them." George Whitefield enthralled great assemblages with his eyes, though they were crippled with strabismus. The Holy Ghost lit them. Many a military chieftain has with a look hurled a regiment to victory or to death. Martin Luther turned his great eye upon an assassin who came to take his life, and the villian fled. Under the glance of the human eye, the tiger, five times a man's strength, snarls back into the African jungle.

Logan Clendening, M.D., who often discusses the diseases of the eye in detail, says that the mechanism of the eye is complicated — and he speaks of the "peculiarities of the sense of vision." Vision is created by light striking on the retina of the eye. The retina is made up of probably the most complicated nerve cells in the entire body. These cells, stimulated by light, carry an impulse of some kind to a special part of the brain where it is translated into form, color and light itself. And yet, this is only part of the mystery of the mechanics of the eye.

For instance, the eye has automatically to close or open the pupil so that exactly the right amount of light comes in. It has to lengthen or shorten the lens so that an object is in focus. Every photographer has learned the trouble that he gets into from similar needs of accommodation with his iris and his distance, and he has had to employ all kinds of gadgets to help him out. Yet, the eye does all of this automatically.

The cells in the retina are of various kinds. Among them, named from their shape, are rods and cones. The present theory is that the cones are stimulated both by light and color perceptions, while the rods perceive only light itself and have nothing to do with color.

The sensation of light produced by radiant energy impinging on the retina consists of two factors — brightness and color. Color is dependent on the wave length, brightness on the intensities of the light rays.

Wonderful sights we see on this earth! — Niagara Falls, where 250,000 cubic feet of water pour over the rocks every second. The moon blossoming like a large jonquil in the garden of the patient stars, or with invisible brush painting a path of silver across seas and lakes, or spreading a silver mantle over the hills and plains of earth. Snow storms glorifying the earth with a covering of white, making the garbage heap look like a king's palace. Square miles of peach blooms kissed by a golden sun. Thousands of fluttering sea gulls' wings. The Grand Canyon, more glorious than words can say, where it seems God paused and worked longer and did better work than in some other places. Ten thousand little children each with a red poppy in hand. Great tall pines, God's million-stringed harp, strung against the wind. But the most wonderful sights we ever see are not so wonderful as the instruments through which we see them — the human eyes.

A poet pictured the sunset and the night in these words:

> The beautiful black stallion men call night
> Hurdles, with one long leap, the sunset bars;
> His flying, wild mane jeweled with a touch of
> lilac light,
> And his graceful cloud-hooves shod with diamond
> stars.

But more wonderful than what is yonder in sunrise morning and sunset evening and midnight splendor are the human eyes that enable us to see these.

Telescope and microscope in one is the human eye. It can see the sun 95,000,000 miles away — and the point of a pin. It can gaze on the smallest insect and the most luminous star. The traveler among the Alps with one glance takes in Mont Blanc and at the next second the face of his watch to see if he has time to climb it. We can from the tip of Mt. Washington take in New England. At night we take into our vision the constellations from horizon to horizon. We can take in at one glance miles of the Mississippi in one second and at the next second tiny dewdrops falling from the rims of lily cups. We sweep into our vision the cloud chariots rolling across the skies and at the next second we take in the earthworm crawling in the mud. Strong enough to behold the "tabernacle of the sun" set in the midst of the heavens and yet so delicate and so semi-infinite that the light coming at the rate of nearly 200,000 miles a second is obliged to halt at the gate of the eye waiting until the portcullus be lifted.

There is not much danger that we shall fail to see the beauties of the landscape by day nor the glories of the heavens by night where the stars blossom in "the infinite meadows of heaven," but there is a danger that we shall be blind to the gold in the common clay of humanity; blind to the opportunities of service; blind to the responsibilities of church; blind to the harvest fields at our doors; blind to the glory and worth of commonplace service; blind to the things that matter most; blind to the warning lights set here and there: blind to the wounded man by the roadside. If the eyes are yielded to God, they are not blind to things of service in the world.

But we have to think of the evil usage of the eyes — because we have learned of the

EVIL EYES

Poets and writers have written many things about the eyes. Note these: "Eyes like a butterfly's gorgeous wings." "Eyes like the reflections of stars in a well." "Eyes like those of a roe tenderly looking at her young." "Eyes like orient pearls." "Eyes like lovely lamps." "Her eyes like marigolds, had sheathed their light, and canopied in darkness sweetly lay, till they might open to adorn the day." "Eyes like torches flinging their beams around." "Sunken grey eyes, like reflections from the aspect of an angel." "Doubting eyes, like a child that never knew but love, whom words of wrath surprise." "Eyes like the summer's light blue sky." "Eyes like the dawn of a day." "Eyes shining like thin skins full of blood." "Twin violets by a shady brook were like her eyes." "Her eyes were homes of silent prayer." "Her eyes are sapphires set in snow." "Honest eyes, blue like tropic skies." "Solar eyes, like meteors which rivel the dark like a new day." "Eyes like blue pansies." "Eyes like the eyes of doves." "Eyes like moonbeams glowing." "Eyes that mock the diamond's blaze." "Eyes mild as a gazelle's." "Limpid eyes laughing in the summer sun." "Eyes dilated as if the spirit world would open before him." "Bright eyes — like lotus blossoms." "Blessed eyes, like a pair of suns, shine in the sphere of smiling." "Eyes whose sleeping lid like snow on violets lies." "Eyes like an orange grove, in whose enchanted bowers the magic fire-flies rove." "Eyes — pioneers that first announce the soft tale of love." "Eyes like the open heaven, holy and pure from sin." "Dim dried eyes like an exhausted well." "Eyes as fair as starbeams among twilight trees." "Eyes like the fish pools in Heshbon, by the gate of Bethlehem." "Deep eyes — darker and softer than the bluest dusk."

But the eye is also spoken of an evil. "Eat thou not the bread of him that hath an evil eye, neither desire thou his dainty meats" (Prov. 23:6). The eyes are oftentimes enemies of the body and the soul. They live and function, creating dangers, as though they had hands to pull up flowers in the soul's garden, as though they were dynamite to blast foundations to bits, as though they were ghouls poisoning wells where thirsty travelers drink.

The truth of the eyes being "instruments of unrighteousness unto sin" (Rom. 6:13) is testified to in the writings of many. For example: "Her eyes worked like an ice gimlet." "Eyes like burnt holes in a blanket." "Eyes like flames of sulfur." "Burning eyes that blaze through a lace veil, like flame through cannon smoke." "The dame had eyes like lightning, or the flash that runs before the hot report of thunder." "Ambiguous . . . eyes like the china dog on the mantel piece." "Expectant yellow eyes, like a cat watching the preparation of a saucer of milk." Balzac says: "His eyes, like those of a pitiless judge." Robert Burton writes: "His eyes are like a balance, apt to propend each way, and to be weighed down with every wench's looks." Joseph Conrad declares: "Those dry eyes of his shining more like poisoned stones than living tissues." And Daudet: "Eyes, gleaming like lizard's eyes in the crevices of old walls." And Emerson: "When a man has base ends, and speaks falsely, the eye is muddy, and sometimes a-squint." And Gautier: "A burning eye, yellow and phosphoric, like the eye of a crocodile." And Holmes: "The lack-lustre eyes, rayless as a Beacon Street door-plate in August." And Keats: "The sophist's eye, like a sharp spear, rent through her utterly, keen, cruel, perceant, stinging." And Sir Thomas Overbury: "Her eyes are like free-booters, living upon the spoil of stragglers." And Saltus: "Eyes — mirage of sultry prisons." And Shakespeare: "And eye like Mara, to threaten and command." And Sterne: "An eye is, for all the world, exactly like a cannon, in this respect, that it is not so much the eye or the cannon, in themselves, as it is in the carriage of the eye and the carriage of the cannon — by which both the one and the other are enabled to do much execution." And Tasso: "His threatening eyes like flaming torches burned." And another: "His eye red as 'twould burn Rome." But weightier than all these are the words of the Bible, showing that the eyes can be enemies of the soul as we have read in Proverbs 23:6: "Eat thou not the bread of him that hath an evil eye, neither desire thou his dainty meats."

And among the seven things that are an abomination unto God the eye is included in the words: "A proud look" (Prov. 6:17).

A brief catalogue of evil eyes is interesting: There is the *winking eye*:

> He that winketh with the eye causeth sorrow (Prov. 10:10).
> Let not them. . .wink with the eye that hate me without a cause (Ps. 35:19).

And *mocking eyes*:

> The eye that mocketh at his father, and despiseth to obey his mother, the ravens of the valley shall pick it out, and the young eagles shall eat it (Prov. 30:17).

And the *insatiate eyes*:

> The eye is not satisfied with seeing (Eccl. 1:8).
> Hell and destruction are never full; so the eyes of man are never satisfied (Prov. 27:20).
> He that hasteth to be rich hath an evil eye (Prov. 28:22).

The insatiate eye is the eye of greed. It becomes yellow, no matter what its color is, from looking too long at gold or its reflection. The unseen, eternal world never enters the vision of insatiate eyes. Desire for gain, search for the seen, forgetting that "a man's life consisteth not in the abundance of the things which he possesseth," no heavenly visions, no holy

communings, no sweet spiritual joys. The spiritual world a
blank — a dense darkness. Miserly eyes that never glow,
that never kindle with luster, fail to achieve one of the highest
uses of the eye — that of being the outward visible sign of a
living soul.

The human eye is an organ of sight but it is also an organ
of speech, and it carries messages to keep, too high for the
voice to utter. The life-giving power of a generous eye,
flashing the quick movement of a sympathetic heart, is well
expressed in Browning's words: "He lived in his mild and
magnificent eye." Even the animals which have no equipment
of distinctively human muscles — those we use to smile with —
nevertheless have the gift of eyes which speak. The human
whose inert and stingy eye holds back like a miser its possible
healing radiance and never speaks the warm glow of the spirit
descends even below the level of the dog and the horse.

Ungenerous eyes are also those which see only a pitiful
fraction of the human and divine scene. Such stingy eyes do
not swing on a pivot like a searchlight; they are set solid
like a lamp post. They see only a groove running in one
direction. They are set solid.

Edwin Arlington Robinson paints a memorable picture of
Aaron Stark, a miser in his line, "with eyes like little
dollars in the dark." Little dollars in the dark — what an
equipment with which to see God's world. And yet how many
people have traded eyes for little dollars.

And *pitiless eyes*:

They shall have no pity on the fruit of the womb; their
eye shall not spare children (Is. 13:18).

His eyes are privily set against the poor (Ps. 10:8).

And *ensnaring eyes* are spoken of when Solomon says:

My son . . . the commandment is a lamp; and the law is
light . . . to keep thee from the evil woman. . . . Lust not after
her beauty in thine heart; neither let her take thee with her
eyelids (Prov. 6:23-25).

And *irreverent eyes*:

> Is this house, which is called by my name, become a den of robbers in your eyes? Behold, even I have seen it, saith the Lord (Jer. 7:11).

> Her priests . . . have put no difference between the holy and profane, neither have they shewed difference between the unclean and the clean, and have hid their eyes from my sabbaths (Ezek. 22:26).

And *jealous eyes*: "And Saul eyed David from that day and forward" (I Sam. 18:9). This has been called the green eye. Shakespeare gave it that name: "Oh, beware, my Lord, of jealousy! It is the green-eyed monster, which doth mock the meat it feeds on." Jesus spoke of the jealous eye when He said: "Is thine eye evil, because I am good?" (Matt. 20:15). Jealous eyes "sear the conscience, warp the judgment, sour the spirit, and blunt all delicate sensibilities." People who look through such eyes bid an eternal farewell to happiness, for "jealousy is as cruel as the grave." Look through jealous eyes — and you will narrow and vitiate your soul.

And the *inflamed eyes of drunkenness*.

> Who hath redness of eyes? They that tarry long at the wine; they that go to seek mixed wine. Look not thou upon the wine when it is red, when it giveth his color in the cup, when it moveth itself aright (Prov. 23:29-31).

All of which means: Keep your eyes off the wine cup, for most sin begins at the eyes. Some sin against the eyes through the stomach.

And *lustful eyes*: the eyes of Potiphar's wife were lustful eyes.

> And it came to pass after these things, that his master's wife cast her eyes upon Joseph; and she said, Lie with me (Gen. 39:7).

Against such eyes, Job warned men when he said:

> I made a covenant with mine eyes; why then should I think upon a maid? (Job 31:1).

So did Peter when he wrote:

> . . . having eyes full of adultery, and that can not cease from sin (II Peter 2:14).

And Job surely had adulterers with lustful eyes in mind when he said:

> They are of those that rebel against the light; they know not the ways thereof, nor abide in the paths thereof. . . . The eye also of the adulterer waiteth for the twilight saying, No eye shall see me: and disguiseth his face (Job 24:13-15).

But God sees. "Doth not he see my ways, and count all my steps?" (Job 31:4). Surely, the lustful eye must often become a painful eye — it dreads the light. The possessor of eyes full of adultery

> hateth the light, neither cometh to the light, lest his deed be reproved. And this is the condemnation, that light is come into the world, and men loved darkness rather than light, because their deeds were evil (John 3:20, 19).

David had lustful eyes when he staked his crown for a woman's caress, when he endangered his throne for a woman's embrace.

> And it came to pass in an eveningtide, that David arose from off his bed, and walked upon the roof of the king's house: and from the roof he saw a woman washing herself; and the woman was very beautiful to look upon (II Sam. 11:2).

Our Lord warned men against the evil of lust when He declared that a look was sometimes tantamount to adultery.

> Ye have heard that it was said by them of old time, Thou shalt not commit adultery: but I say unto you, That whosoever looketh on a woman to lust after her hath committed adultery with her already in his heart (Matt. 5:27-28).

What a curse to a man to look out upon the world through eyes of lust. All life seems an inflamed and unholy thing. The light that comes in through adulterous eyes wears a foul track across the brain and induces a fever in the heart which nothing but a miracle can remove. There is only one alchemy which can change the eyes of lust into eyes that are pure — the blood of Jesus which cleanses from all sin.

And not least, though we mention them last, among evil eyes are *fault-finding eyes*. Jesus knew this when He said,

> And why beholdest thou the mote that is in thy brother's eye, but considerest not the beam that is in thine own eye?

Or how wilt thou say to thy brother, Let me pull out the mote out of mine eye; and, behold, a beam is in thine own eye? Thou hypocrite, first cast out the beam out of thine own eye; and then shalt thou see clearly to cast out the mote out of thy brother's eye (Matt. 7:3-5).

Lowell calls them "flaw-finding eyes, like needle points." Fault-finding eyes that are eyes of malice, and eyes that snap with ill will, eyes that magnify faults, eyes that dim merit, eyes that see only defects, eyes that see blemishes.

Jesus showed how important it is that we yield our eyes to God as instruments of righteousness when He said:

The light of the body is the eye: if therefore thine eye be single, thy whole body shall be full of light. But if thine eye be evil, thy whole body shall be full of darkness. If therefore the light that is in thee be darkness, how great is that darkness! (Matt. 6 22-23).

You will recall how Bunyan represents the five senses as five gates to the citadel, all of them barred against Emmanuel, their rightful King. So it is with him that hath an evil eye. Evil eyes that read wrong things — how they serve the Devil. How often the eyes are made sewer channels that carry slop and garbage and plague to souls. Books as foul as filth are read — books which ought never to see light. I do not mean that all books should be religious. There are good books, good histories, good biographies, good novels, good books of all styles to fill the minds of the young so that there will be no more room for the useless and the vicious than there is for chaff in dough. But "I am a business man and have no time to examine what my children read — no time to inspect the books that come into my house." If your children were threatened with typhoid, would you have time to go for the doctor? Would you have time to watch the progress of the disease? Would you have time for the funeral?

In the presence of God, I warn you that your children are threatened with moral and spiritual typhoid and that unless the thing be stopped, it will be to them a funeral of body, a

funeral of mind, a funeral of soul — three funerals in a day.
Evil eyes that look on bad pictures — how they please the
Devil and dishonor God. Evil eyes that look lustfully on
women — how they please Satan and grieve God. Evil eyes
that never see open church doors — how they gratify Satan
and displease God. Evil eyes that covet what others have
— how they please Satan! Evil eyes to which the shine of
gold means more than sunlight and moonlight and heaven's
light.

I want us to think of the truth that through the eyes come

The Blessings of Light

"Let there be light!" said God. And there was light.
What a wonderful thing light is! But not to the blind people.
The light of the glowworm, the firefly, the cat's eye; the light
of boiling lava in deep volcanic craters, of phosphorus; comet's
tails millions of miles in length, showers, of meteors, of the
sun, the dawning light of morning, the fading light of evening, of moon hanging like a globe in the sky, of the moons
of all the planets, of rings of Jupiter, of Pluto, the newly
discovered planet; lights red and green in railroad systems,
candlelight, lamplight, incandescent light. Light of beacon
lights, searchlights, conflagration, bonfires, forest fires, molten
metal, furnaces, strange lights of laboratories, sparks that
ride with the blast, burning charcoal, blacksmith's forge, flash-
lights, burning blubber in Eskimo's icy cave, beautiful bowls
in Mohammedan mosques, incense sticks that burn before
images of Buddha, decorating homes of India at time of Dewali
festival, fishing boats of China sea, lights of sparks that
scatter from wheels of friction, of phosphorescent ocean wave,
of miner's lamps, of aurora borealis, of my hearth when the log
is the vista of my dreams, of my hearth when glowing coals
become an avenue for memory, of my hearth when dreams
are done and memory is fast asleep, of the spark found by
stirring ashes in the morning.

God said: "Let there be light." And without eyes we could enjoy none of the lights that are in this world. What a wonderful thing to have sight — to have functioning eyes.

But we might be blessed if we considered the

LIMITATIONS OF THE EYES

Though the eyes are wonderful — microscopes and telescopes in one, superior organs of the human body — still they have their limitations. The microscope that enables us to see a world in a drop of water authenticates such a statement. The telescope, magnifying the power of the human eye millions of times and enabling us to view landscapes millions of miles away, testifies to the limitations of human eyes. The spectograph which makes it so that human eyes can see the constituent elements of the remotest astral bodies — the gold in the sun, the copper in Mars, the iron in the moons of Jupiter — shows us the limitations of man's eyes. The X-ray, without which we can not see the marrow in men' bones or the pounding of the heart, authenticates all asseverations as to the limitations of the human eyes.

We know that of all the senses sight is supreme. Sight, with the instrument of the eye, has not a superior beneath this dome of skull and brain. But sight, through the instruments of the eyes, cannot see everything. The eyes cannot see thought. The eyes cannot see love. The eyes cannot see hope. The eyes cannot see faith. The eyes cannot see prayer.

But, forgetting those higher matters for a moment and coming back to the physical things, the eyes, up to 458,000,000,000 vibrations per second, cannot see anything at all. And light waves have to beat in upon the eye at the rate of 727,000,000,000 vibrations per second before they can see ultra violet. And we cannot say what goes on beyond the vibrations which produce ultra violet.

And the eyes cannot see eternal things. The eyes cannot see the forces that govern the physical world. All these forces are unseen. You never saw heat, nor wind, nor electricity, nor gravitation, nor life. You never saw ambition, nor aspiration, nor personal influence, nor pain, nor music, nor love, nor prayer, nor emotion, nor decision, nor degeneration, nor death.

While we look not at the things which are seen, but at the things which are not seen; for the things which are seen are temporal; but the things which are not seen are eternal (II Cor. 4:18).

How great the truth:

> While with an eye made quiet by power
> Of harmony, and the deep power of joy,
> We see into the life of things.

Moses "endured — as seeing him who is invisible."

But think now of the

BLIGHT OF BLINDNESS

How wonderful the blessings of sight. How awful to be blind — never to see a child's face, a starlit night, a flower, an orchard. Never to see anything. What a blight to be forever in midnight! How long was the night for the man born blind, and for blind Bartimaeus — until Jesus came along. Terrible to be blind — "blind as hooded falcons," "blind as the monologue of a storm," "blind as a pilot beaten sightless by foam," "blind like tragic marks of stone," "blind as Samson at the mills of the Philistines," "blind as Zedekiah in Babylon."

Think of Samson losing his eyesight!

> But the Philistines took him, and put out his eyes, and brought him down to Gaza, and bound him with fetters of brass; and he did grind in the prison house (Judg. 16:21).

This terrible loss Samson bewailed in his last pathetic prayer.

> And Samson called unto the Lord, and said, O Lord God, remember me, I pray thee, and strengthen me, I pray thee, only this once, O God, that I may be at once avenged of the Philistines for my two eyes (Judg. 16:28).

How terrible this scene in the Bible:

> And they slew the sons of Zedekiah before his eyes, and put out the eyes of Zedekiah, and bound him with fetters of brass, and carried him to Babylon (II Kings 25:7).

But more terrible than to be born blind or to be made sightless is to have two good eyes and yet be blind! Listen to the Psalmist:

> They have mouth: but they speak not: eyes have they, but they see not (Ps. 115:5).

Hearken to these words:

> For the heart of this people is waxed gross, and their ears are dull of hearing, and their eyes have they closed; lest they should see with their eyes, and hear with their ears, and understand with their heart, and should be converted, and I should heal them (Acts 28:27).

Blind eyes, speaking of minds blinded by a veil of prejudice and unbelief. Blind eyes, testifying to minds contracted as when bigotry narrows visual power!

More awful than blindness is it to have two good eyes and yield them to the Devil as instruments of unrighteouness, so that perspective and localizing power is destroyed, so that spiritual things are distorted as would be a landscape if looked at through a badly twisted pane of glass.

Thinking of the blight and burden of blindness, let me ask you a few questions: What if God were suddenly to take your eyes out of their sockets? What would you promise God to do with your eyes if He would give them back? If God would ask you to read the Bible daily, if He would restore your eyesight, would you? If God would require of you the promise to look upon the preacher in the pulpit and hear his sermon each Sunday, would you promise that to get your eyes back? If God would say you could not get your eyes back unless you promised to visit someone in the name of Jesus, would you promise to visit? If your eyes were torn from their sockets and God would tell you He would put them back, even as Jesus healed the severed ear of Malchus, if you would pay God His one-tenth henceforth, would you promise to do so? I think you would. How much more then should you, in gratitude for your eyes, do these things?

But I want to think now of the blessed truth that

GOD HAS SOMETHING MORE LOVELY FOR HIS
CHILDREN THAN EYES HAVE EVER YET SEEN

But as it is written, Eye hath not seen, nor hath ear heard, neither have entered into the heart of man, the things which God hath prepared for them that love him (I Cor. 2:9).

Oh, why will men be content with lives so small, when God means them to be so large? Why will they cramp themselves in their contemptible little worldly plans, when God is waiting to flood them with His own eternity? "The things which are seen are temporal." "They are born of time. They last with time. They will pass with the passing of time. But the things which are not seen are eternal."

Perhaps no woman ever lived to whom the world offered more than it gave to Madame Pompadour, mistress of Louis XIV, and the most powerful woman of her day. In her diary, she wrote: "I am always gloomy. The King's kindness affects me no longer. I have lost relish for all that once pleased me. I caused my house at Paris to be furnished magnificently. That pleased me for two days. My residence at Bellview is charming — and I alone can not endure it. In a word, I do not live. I am dead before my time."

Something like that Catherine of Russia said, when she came to die: "I am an accumulation of broken ends."

On the night before the conquest of Quebec, General Wolfe lay in his tent reciting:

> The boast of heraldry, the pomp of power,
> And all that beauty, all that wealth e'er gave,
> Await alike that inevitable hour,
> The paths of glory lead but to the grave.

Wolfe was killed next morning. And for us all "this earthly house of our tabernacle" shall soon "be dissolved." But when our tent blows down, if Jesus tarry, "we shall have a building of God, a house not made with hands, eternal in the heavens" — a house we have never seen. It is eternal!

Thank God for the glorious and good things our eyes have

seen! Temporal. Thank God for the most glorious things our eyes have *not* seen! Eternal. All the flowers our eyes have seen here will fade, but not the eternal flowers over there. All the trees our eyes have seen here will fall, but not the tree of life over there. All the streams our eyes have seen here will dry up, but the stream that flows from the throne, never. All the faces our eyes will see here will fade, doubtless. But faces glorified with eternal radiance and beauty over there — never!

We ought not to say so much of the human eyes without thinking of

GOD'S EYES

"He that formed the eye, shall he not see?" Job asked: "Doth not he see all my ways and count all my footsteps?" "Thou God seest me."

> But the land, whither ye go to possess it, is a land of hills and valleys, and drinketh water of the rain of heaven: a land which the Lord thy God careth for: the eyes of the Lord thy God are always upon it, from the beginning of the year even unto the end of the year (Deut. 11:11-12).

> For the eyes of the Lord run to and fro throughout the whole earth, to shew himself strong in the behalf of them whose heart is perfect toward him. Herein thou hast done foolishly: therefore from henceforth thou shalt have wars (II Chron. 16:9).

> The eyes of the Lord are in every place, beholding the evil and the good (Prov. 15:3).

How foolish men are to think to hide from God to whom the midnight is as the noonday, to whom the darkness and the light are both alike.

Job showed the folly of such evil in these words:

> The eye also of the adulterer waiteth for the twilight, saying, No eye shall see me: and disguiseth his face (Job 24:15).

And God, who seeth all, who knows our downsitting and uprising, makes a promise to those who yield the members of their bodies to Him as instruments of righteousness:

> He that walketh righteously, and speaketh uprightly; he that

despiseth the gain of oppressions, that shaketh his hands from holding of bribes, that stoppeth his ears from hearing of blood, and shutteth his eyes from seeing evil; he shall dwell on high: his place of defence shall be the munitions of rocks: bread shall be given him; his waters shall be sure (Is. 33:15-16).

And God says: "I will guide thee with mine eye."

Precious promise God hath given
  To the weary passerby,
On the way from earth to Heaven,
  "I will guide thee with mine eye."

When temptations almost win thee,
  And thy trusted watchers fly,
Let this promise ring within thee,
  "I will guide thee with mine eye."

When thy secret hopes have perished
  In the grave of years gone by,
Let this promise still be cherished,
  "I will guide thee with mine eye."

When the shades of life are falling,
  And the hour has come to die,
Hear the trusty Pilot calling,
  "I will guide thee with mine eye."

"I will guide thee, I will guide thee,
  I will guide thee with mine eye;
On the way from earth to heaven,
  I will guide thee with mine eye."

And I beg you by the eyes of Jesus that always looked with compassion on the multitudes, that sometimes flared with the wrath of Heaven's hatred of sin, that sometimes wept tears of grief over cities which shut God out — let your eyes be in God's calling and in God's keeping as instruments of righteousness. By the mercy and grace that were in the eyes of Jesus when, on the night of Peter's base denial, He turned and looked on Peter, I beg you to let God use your eyes. By the solemnity of the thought of God's all-seeing eye, by the knowledge that the darkness is as the noonday with Him with whom we have

to do, by the promise of Him who says "I will guide thee
with mine eye," by the uncertainty of life and the certainty
of death, by the shortness of time and the endless reach of
eternity, by the certainty of that hour when you must look
into the eyes of Jesus, the righteous Judge, I beg you to yield
your eyes to God as instruments of righteousness.

Remember the words in Luke 11:34-36:

> The light of the body is the eye: therefore when thine eye is
> single, thy whole body is full of light; but when thine eye is
> evil, thy body also is full of darkness. Take heed therefore
> that the light which is in thee be not darkness.

Get warning and comfort in the words:

> For the eyes of the Lord run to and fro throughout the
> whole earth, to shew himself strong in the behalf of them whose
> heart is perfect toward him (II Chron. 16:9).

Let it never be said of you that you have an evil eye (Mark
7:22). And rejoice in God's promise:

> He that walketh righteously, and speaketh uprightly; he that
> despiseth the gain of oppressions, that shaketh his hands from
> holding of bribes, that stoppeth his ears from hearing of blood,
> and shutteth his eyes from seeing evil; he shall dwell on high:
> his place of defence shall be the munitions of rocks: bread
> shall be given him; his waters shall be sure (Is. 33:15-16).

Chapter Three

THE EARS OF THE HUMAN BODY

He that planted the ear, shall he not hear? (Ps.
94:9).
The hearing ear . . . the Lord hath made (Prov. 20:12).
*Yet hear the word of the Lord, O ye women, and let
your ear receive the word of his mouth* (Jer. 9:20).
So that thou incline thine ear unto wisdom (Prov. 2:2).
He that hath ears to hear, let him hear (Matt. 11:15).

In his letter to the church at Corinth, Paul, knowing that
the body is the essential instrument by which the soul lives its
life here below, refers to the body as the temple of the Holy
Ghost.

What? know ye not that your body is the temple of the Holy
Ghost which is in you, which ye have of God, and ye are
not your own? (I Cor. 6:19).

Then he shows that the Christian's business is to glorify God.

For ye are bought with a price: therefore glorify God in your
body, and in your spirit, which are God's (I Cor. 6:20).

On one of the walls in the Library of Congress is this
inscription: "There is but one temple in the universe, and
that is the body of man." Carlyle said: "Whoso layeth his
hand on a human body, toucheth heaven."

The Bible eulogizes the body; and Christ, teaching the
superior value of the soul, warning men against the danger of
placing more honor on the body than the soul, did, by His
incarnation, by His being "made flesh," show the dignity of
the human body; did thus rebuke the spurious philosophies
and speculations of the early Gnostics who taught that "our

39

spirits become polluted and miserable only in consequence of their habitation in flesh," who taught that "the fall of man was only the inevitable result of the union of the spirit with the body," who taught that "the body was the pure badge of the spirit's dishonor." Against this, the Apostle John mightily protests when he says of Jesus, "The Word was made flesh." How diametrically opposite, moreover, is Plato's estimate of the human body — "Whoso layeth his hand on a human body toucheth necessary evil" — and the estimate of the writer of the Hebrews who, speaking of Christ, said:

> Wherefore when he cometh into the world, he saith, Sacrifice and offering thou wouldest not, but a body hast thou prepared me (Heb. 10:5).

How in antithesis, too, the teaching of him who avoided all mention of the date or locality of his birth, Plotinus, a disciple of Plato, who refused to permit his picture to be taken, or painted, because it would "unduly perpetuate the image of a body he abominated," and the teaching of Paul who said that the body was the temple of the Holy Ghost. How came two geniuses, almost contemporaries, to make such different statements about the dignity of the human body? Paul believed in the incarnation. Plotinus did not. "The Word was made flesh." Then the body, consecrated by the personal habitation of the Godhead, is something honorable in the universe of God. David said: "I am fearfully and wonderfully made." And Shakespeare, amazed at the grandeur of man's nervous system, thinking of the construction of our eyes, pondering the adjustment of our ears, marveling at the manifestation of our fingers, giving thought to the pendulation of our limbs and the beating of the human body's heart, amazed at the wonders of the human ear, said:

> What a piece of work is man!
> How noble in reason. How infinite
> in faculty!
> In form and moving how express
> and admirable;

In action how like an angel!
In apprehension how like a god!

Since the believer's body is a member of Christ, that body must not be used for an unholy purpose. It must be used to manifest the holiness of Christ. It must be used in devotion to Him.

> I beseech you therefore, brethren, by the mercies of God, that ye present your bodies a living sacrifice, holy, acceptable unto God, which is your reasonable service (Rom. 12:1).

No one can accept the fact that God really wants to use our bodies through which His own life and love is manifest to the world without that acceptance having a tremendous influence on his manner of living. I know, however, that there are those who formally accept these statements that the Scriptures make about the body and still live on as thoughtlessly as a dog in his kennel, a pig in his sty, or a fattening steer in his feeding stall. As the body, so the soul, says Shakespeare:

> There's nothing ill can dwell in such a temple:
> If the ill spirit have so fair a house,
> Good things will strive to dwell with it.

As the soul, so the body, says Spenser:

> So every spirit, as it is more pure,
> And hath in it the more of heavenly light,
> So it the fairer body doth procure
> To habit in, and it more fairly dight,
> With cheerful grace and amiable sight.
> For, of the soul, the body form doth take,
> For the soul is form, and doth the body make.

And Emerson confirms the thrust of both utterances:

> A broken complexion, a swinish look, ungenerous acts, and the want of due knowledge — all blab. Can a cook, a Chiffinch, an Iachimo be mistaken for Zeno or Paul? Confucius exclaimed, "How can a man be concealed! How can a man be concealed!"

Thinking of the body, Paul says: "Let not sin reign in your mortal body" (Rom. 6:12). Sin, making life incoherent,

plunging man into a gloom that ever deepens, into a restless-
ness that ever increases, into a remorse that will not be hushed,
is full of heavy liabilities. As to the body, sin — the curse of
all curses, the quintessence of all horrors, the causative
element of all world suffering — is ever a seed big with future
pain and grief.

As saith the poet:

> For beauty's gesture and her loom of light,
> For starry reason and for manly might,
> Sin gives the skulking step, the furtive eye,
> The curse, the groan, the death that can not die.

Sad, full of warning, wise words for us to heed, are these
words which Thomas Watson wrote in the fifteenth Century:

> I think the immortal servants of mankind,
> Who, from their graves watch by how slow degrees,
> The World-soul greatens with the centuries,
> Mourn most man's barren levity of mind,
> The ear to no grave harmonies inclined,
> The witless thirst for false wits worthless leer,
> The laugh mistimed in tragic presences,
> The eye to all majestic meanings blind.

Thinking upon these things we see how necessary it is that
we yield our ears to God as instruments of righteousness —
so that our testimony can be what Shakespeare wrote:

> For know, my heart stands armied in mine ear
> And will not let a false sound enter there.

Kindred truth spoke Voltaire, who said: "The ear is the road
to the heart." Ears yielded to God as instruments of righteousness will, as the Bible says, be "opened to discipline," will
"bow down to God's understanding," will "hear the reproof
of life," will "bow down to the words of the wise," will not
be "heavy that they can not hear," will not be, as the poet
says, "like a mildewed ear, blasting its wholesome brother."

In "Paradise Lost," Milton pictures an angel called Uriel
being sent down from heaven to look in the garden of Eden
for the Devil. He represents this angel with a wand in his
hand, moving about the garden, but he can see Satan nowhere.

At length he sees a toad lying in the ear of Eve. He touches the toad with the tip of his hand — and out springs Satan. The thought is that the Devil has captured the ear of the race and expects to hold it. And he will do it until some day the sinner hears the voice of the Son of God, and is made alive in Him.

The two senses — seeing and hearing — are prominent everywhere. Two of the principal arts — music and painting — are developed by them. Music is useless if there be no ears to hear it; and paintings are worthless if there be no eyes to see them. Seeing and hearing form a large part of our railroad systems, the signals for the sight, and the whistle and the bell for the ear. And at every crossing the traveler is halted by a sign board calling upon him to look and listen. The major portion of our intelligence we get through seeing and hearing. And if the Gospel would win its way to the uttermost parts of the earth, it must accommodate itself to these two senses — the printed page for the eye and the voice of testimony for the ear.

But of the ears we speak now. Think of the

WONDERS OF THE EARS

Could any other but God conceive it? Could any other but God plan it? Could any other but God build it? Could any other but God fully understand it?

Washington's monument, with its many stair steps, have men and women climbed. Stone gables of mountain heights have men with daring and careful feet scaled. The gloomy recesses of Mammoth Cave and other caves of earth into which no ray of sunlight or starlight enters, have men explored. The depths of the coral parlors of the ocean have men sounded. The finest marble mausoleums of earth have men admired. The dim aisles of glorious cathedrals have men reverently walked. The solemn grandeur of pyramidic grotto have men invaded. The dusty bandages of mummies sleeping in the dust of centuries have men disturbed. Some tombs, like the tomb of King Tut, have men ransacked. Underground passage ways adorned with stalactite and stalagmite, have men wandered through.

But like no palace stairway man ever ascended, like no labyrinth of intricate passage ways ever explored, like no fairyland of wonder is the human ear. More wonderful than any arch man ever lifted, more wonderful than any transept window man ever illuminated, more wonderful than any musical instrument with which man builds rhythmic palaces of melody, more wonderful than any Corinthian column man ever "adorned with lily work," more wonderful than any Gothic cloister men ever elaborated, more glorious than primeval forest ever pierced by pioneer, more interesting than "dislocated writing that looks like a profile drawing of the Sierra Nevadas," is the human ear.

Yes, more mystifying the ear than any circular stairway ever created, more majestic the ear than any stone gable ever placed, more mysterious the ear than any shell home of sea fish, more interesting the ear than any petaled rose — and as romantic the ear "as any Bouguereau canvas." Yes, again I say, more intricate the human ear than the embroidery on a kings' mantle, more surpassing in beauty than the skilled workmanship of the sculptor who "raises children unto God from the sterile womb of stone," more enticing for study than the Urim and Thummin of the breastplate, or the gold ephod bound to the shoulders of the priest with wreathen chains.

Now 256 vibrations per second produce what musicians call the middle C note on the piano. Up to 9,000 vibrations per second — or 24,000 at the most — the ear still registers sound. And Mr. Huxley said that if our ears were keen enough we could hear the flowers grow. And George Eliot thought we should then die of the roar on the other side of the silence.

What is the human ear — "mysterious home of reverberation and echo"? Talmadge called it a Grand Central Depot of

Sound — headquarters, to which quick dispatches come, part
of the way by bone, part of the way by cartilege, part of the
way by nerve, the slowest dispatch plunging into the ear at
the rate of 1,090 feet per second.

What is the ear — with its grotesque contrivances? It has
been called "a small musical instrument on which is played
all the music you ever hear" — "from the grandeurs of the
August thunderstorm to the softest breathing of a flute." And
the delicacy of this instrument of music — only one quarter of
an inch of surface and the thinness of one two hundred and
fiftieth of an inch, and that thinness divided into three layers —
has God's signature written all over it.

What is the human ear? A wise man said it is a bridge
leading from the outside natural world to the inside spiritual
world — we being able to see the abutment at this end but
the fog of an uplifted mystery hiding the abutment at the
the rate of 1,090 feet per second.

What is the ear? We agree with him who called it the
whispering gallery of the soul. Dr. Allen says: "The average
piano has a keyboard with eighty-eight keys. But you have a
keyboard with fifteen hundred keys in each ear. The ear is
so sensitive that, in a completely sound-proof room, you can
actually hear the blood flowing through your vessels."

The marvel of the external ear! Capable of catching 73,700
vibrations per second, this external ear takes in all kinds of
sounds — from the solemn groan of dying thunder on the
distant wind to the irritating buzz of a fly, or the soft whispers
of a sleeping baby's breathing.

Marvel at the external ear, adorned in all ages by precious
stones, which is a precisely dressed porter ushering in
thousands of sounds and sound waves in a day, some sound
waves coming with noisy clamor and some coming gently like
the glistening dew or falling light.

Marvel, as you imagine you can step inside the ear as a

dwarf steps inside a palace, at the wonders of what goes on in the middle ear. After entering the outer ear, sound waves pass inward, reaching the middle ear, which is a little cavity in the temporal bone of the skull. The cavity is shaped like a drum, and is often called the tympanum, or ear drum. At the inner end of the auditory canal is the tympanic membrane. This stretches like a piece of thin skin across the bottom of the canal, and separates the external ear from the tympanum. The cavity of the tympanum is filled with air. Sound smites this drum and it trembles! The message is taken from the drum by those marvelous little bones called, because of their grotesque shapes, the hammer, the anvil, the stirrup. Then the stirrup, agitated by this news from the outer court of things, knocks at a little window and is hospitably received. But the sound is in a hurry to reach the brain. And so it is taken from this mysterious window by a tiny pool of water, just beyond it. And then waves from that microscopic pool of water are the elf-like fingers that play that many stringed instrument. At this point the nerves — wondrous nerves, marvelous nerves — quivering with news from time and eternity, take up the message and pass it on to the brain.

Now let us think of the

ENJOYMENT THE EARS AFFORD AND OF
THE DEPRIVATION OF DEAFNESS

Talmadge said that the human voice — capable of producing 17,592,186,044,415 sounds, and all that variety made, not for the regalement of beast and bird, but for the human ear — was God's eulogy to the human ear. He speaks, saying:

> For the ear everything mellifluous, from the birth hour when our earth was wrapped in swaddling clothes of light and serenaded by other worlds, from the time when Jubal thrummed the first harp and pressed a key of the first organ down to the music of this Sabbath morning. Yea, for the ear the coming overtures of heaven, for whatever other part of the body may

be left in the dust, the ear, we know, is to come to celestial
life; otherwise, why the 'harpers harping with their harps'?

Then Talmadge tells of how men have attempted to master
the human ear, and "gain supremacy over this gate of the immortal soul." He says:

Great battles were fought by Mozart, Gluck, and Weber, and
by Beethoven and Meyerbeer, by Rossini and by all the roll of
German and Italian and French composers, some of them in the
battle leaving their blood on the keynotes and the musical scores.
Great battle fought for the ear — fought with baton, with organ
pipe, with trumpet, with cornet-a-piston, with all ivory and
brazen and silver and golden weapons of the orchestra; royal
theatre and cathedral and academy of music the fortresses of
the contest for the ear. England and Egypt fought for the
supremacy of the Suez Canal, and the Spartans and the
Persians fought for the defile at Thermopylae, but the
musicians of all ages have fought for the mastery of the
auditory canal and the defile of the immortal soul and the
Thermopylae of struggling cadences.

"For the conquest of the ear, Haydn struggled on up from
the garret where he had neither fire nor food, on and on until
under the too great nervous strain of hearing his own oratorio
of the *Creation* performed, he was carried out to die, but
leaving as his legacy to the world 118 symphonies, 163 pieces
for the baritone, 15 masses, 5 oratorios, 42 German and Italian
songs, 39 canons, 365 English and Scotch songs with accompani-
ment, and 1536 pages of libretti. All that to capture the gate
of the body that swings in from the tympanum to the "snail
shell" lying on the beach of the ocean of the immortal soul.

"To conquer the ear, Handel struggled on from the time
when his father would not let him go to school lest he learn the
gamut and become a musician, and from the time, when he
was allowed in the organ loft just to play, after the audience
had left, one voluntary, to the time when he left to all nations
his unparalleled oratorios of *Esther, Deborah, Samson, Jephthah,
Judas Maccabeus, Israel in Egypt, and The Messiah,* the soul
of the great German composer still weeping in the Dead March
of our great obsequies and triumphing in the raptures of every
Easter morn.

"To conquer the ear and take this gate of the immortal soul,
Schubert composed his great *Serenade,* writing the staves of the

music on the bill of fare in a restaurant, and went on until he
could leave as a legacy to the world over a thousand magnificent
compositions in music. To conquer the ear and take this gate of
the soul's castle Mozart struggled on through poverty until he
came to a pauper's grave, and one chilly wet afternoon the
body of him who gave to the world the *Requiem* and the *G-
minor Symphony* was brunched in on the top of two other
paupers into a grave which to thi day is epitaphless.

Thinking upon this we learn something of how great is the
deprivation of deafness. How terrible to be deaf. Since for the
ear all musical instruments were made, what a deprivation
never to hear a mocking bird, the Beethoven of the boughs;
never to hear a quail whistle his bob-white call; never to hear
the dash of rain on a roof; never to hear the roar of ocean's
waves; never to hear the doxology of worshipful assembly;
never to hear a flute or organ or clarinet or bell or bassoon
or choir or soloist or laughter. Never to hear music or chimes
or an orchestra! What deprivation! No wonder some one
called the ear "the great Giant's Causeway for the monarchs of
music to pass over"!

But a worse tragedy than to be deaf it is have two good
ears keenly sensitized to every sound and voice and yet have
ears such as the Psalmist mentions: "Their poison is like the
poison of a serpent: they are like the deaf adder that stoppeth
her ear (Ps. 58:4).

How tragic the deprivations of deafness found among people!
But more tragic for people to be found guilty under the
indictment found in the Proverbs: "A wicked doer giveth heed
to false lips; and a liar giveth ear to a naughty tongue" (Prov.
17:4).

How terrible to be deaf — deaf as the ears of the Sphinx!
But more terrible to have ears that are disobedient and
rebellious, rebellious at the voice of rebuke and truth, disobedient to God's voice of love and wisdom and invitation,
deaf to the cry of the poor and needy. Men dishonor God
not through physically deaf and dead ears but through ears

normal — ears pleased with vulgarity and tickled with the tale bearer's talk, which joy in the gossip's hurtful gossip. How Satan, the infernal enemy of our souls, is pleased when people yield their ears to be willing receptacles for dirty language, blasphemy, profanity, lying, deceitful declarations! That makes us to add Thackeray's words: "Let him that hath ears stuff them with cotton."

Wise it is to have our ears cut off, as Peter cut off the ear of Malchus, than to give ear to Satan. How we need to remember these words:

> The ear that heareth the reproof of life abideth among the wise (Prov. 15:31).
>
> As an earring of gold, and an ornament of fine gold, so is a wise reprover upon an obedient ear (Prov. 25:12).

How we need to have ears that are yielded to God as instruments of righteousness — ears opened by the Lord (Ps. 40:6), ears that incline themselves to the words of God's mouth (Ps. 78:1), ears that bow themselves to the understanding of wisdom, ears that are the ears of the wise that seek knowledge, ears that turn not away from hearing God's law, ears that, when gospel sermons are preached, find not these sermons "as tedious as a twice told tale, vexing the ears of a drowsy man," ears that "listen to the voice of God, no matter how or when or where it comes."

Dr. Gordon asks, speaking of hearing: "Are your ears keen — the ears of your mind, your heart, your spirit? Do you not know that our actions and lives take on the quality of our hearing? God has five voices with which He speaks to us — the outer voice of nature, the inner voice of conscience, the intimate voice of circumstances, the tender voice of the babe when you are in its presence, the plain and unmistakable voice in the Bible. How keen and responsive is our hearing?"

"They have ears to hear, and hear not" (Ezek. 12:2). "Bring forth . . . the deaf that have ears" (Is. 43:8). "Hear, O Israel, the statutes and judgments which I speak in your ears" (Deut. 5:1). "Hear . . . my declaration with your ears" (Job 13:17). "Blessed are . . . your ears for they hear" (Matt. 13:16). Listen to the voice of God's Word. "He that hath an ear, let him hear what the Spirit saith unto the churches."

Do you have ears to hear when the Bible speaks and when saved men speak and when people who love God speak of what the grace of God can do for the lost? Not what environment, not what psychology, not what philosophy, not what political schemes, not what sociology, not what science can do, but what the grace of God can do. How God is glorified through our ears and how the Devil is shamed through our ears when we incline our ears to listen to God and turn deaf ears to Satan.

O for men with ears deaf to the voice of the Devil. O for men with ears open to the voice of God. Let him that hath ears, hear what *God* saith. And do what *God* commandeth. And go the direction that *God* pointeth. And hate the things *God* hates. And love the things *God* loves.

What an evil thing it is to have, when spiritual matters are in the balance, what the Bible calls "dull ears" or "itching ears" or "uncircumcised ears" or "rebellious ears" — and to be found among those of whom Paul speaks who "turn away their ears from the truth" (II Tim. 4:4).

Now I would take time to warn you against the usage or nonusage of your ears that will prove your kinship to the wicked

I — HEAR FAMILY

Members of this family turn away their ears from the truth. Beware of the I-Hear folks. These are they who, their ears open to gossip, hear all that is going and keep going all that is heard. Know them? They hear what is talked and talk what they hear. They hear here, there, everywhere. They hear what was, what is, what shall be. They hear what cannot be, what ought not to be, and what should be. They hear the possible and the impossible, the visionary and the real, the utopian and the practicable. They hear the result of all events, the beginning and the end of all happenings. They hear often. Then hear much. They hear by day; they hear by night. They hear everything, all the time. Each of them hears. All of them hear.

The I-Hear folks never use ear trumpets, but they trumpet all the gossip they hear. In telling what they hear, they can take a square acre of silence and speak their voices all over it. They have ears for the voices of slanderers — wicked slanderers who, in their gossip about others, would slander the sun, murder the moon, accuse the stars, and throw ink on the rainbow.

The I-Hear people hear all the hearsay that is abroad — and keep abroad all the hearsay, uniting naughty tongues with evil ears. What is spoken in the closet they hear and repeat from the housetop. What is spoken once in private they hear and tell twice in public. What is made known behind closed doors, they make public property. What is painted in the dark with few eyes to see they picture in the light for all eyes to behold. The likelihood is that they will never become deaf. A pity, some think.

Hearers of rumors, they spread rumors. Hearers of reports, they manufacture evil reports. Rather perverse themselves, they twist things out of shape. Frequently they hear things altogether as things are not. Hearing, they invert. Hearing, they alter. Hearing, they invent. Hearing, they make the numerator greater than it ought to be and the denominator smaller than it should be. Happenings that take place in the cellar, they hear occurred in the parlor. Understand?

If so, you understand that this family does not hear aright. And so understanding, you understand aright. Straight things these I-Hears make crooked and crooked things crookeder. White they make black and black blacker. Sweet they make bitter and the bitter bitterer. Good they make bad and bad worse. Herein is the iniquity of their hearing discovered. Hearing wild rumors they, delighting in the sensational, make the rumors wilder. Hearing of ant hills of transgression, they, pleased with exaggeration, make these ant hills mountains of unpardonable iniquity. Hearing uncertain and shadowy reports, they, wickedly definite, establish these in the ears of others. Hearing of trivial affairs, they declare boldly that upon these trivial affairs "the whole law hangeth and the prophets."

They hear all that happened, happens, and shall happen — and a little more. Hearing evil reports, they use the plus sign. Hearing good reports concerning those who merit praise and deserve honor, they put the minus sign into operation. Thus do their tongues and ears work in unison — diabolically.

And now let us think of

God's Ears

"He that planted the ear, shall he not hear?" God who gave us the ear hears all voices — in earth, in sea, in sky — all voices everywhere, all sounds of the universe. God hears all voices — man's voice in song or prayer or profanity. God hears the voices of all beasts and birds — the lion roaring in the jungle and the eagle screaming in flight toward its prey. Our laughter God hears. Our whispers God hears. The cry of the prisoner in the dungeon at midnight God hears. God who created man's ears, has ears. He hears — hears all we say.

We are told that Jupiter of Crete was always represented in statuary and painting as without ears — suggesting that he did not want to be bothered with the affairs of the world. But not so our God. His ears are open to the cry of the needy.

> The eyes of the Lord are upon the righteous, and his ears are open unto their cry (Ps. 34:15).

His ears hear the words of oppression.

> Lord, bow down thine ear, and hear: open, Lord, thine

eyes, and see: and hear the words of Sennacherib, which hath
sent him to reproach the living God (II Kings 19:16).

What encouragement to know God hears the cry of the penitent, that God hears our prayers. What a terror for us to
know that God hears all our evil words. What a comfort to
know that God hears the soft flowing of our tears and the sobs
of our grief. He hears the prisoner's sigh. He hears the dying
syllables of wounded soldiers and shipwrecked sailors. He
hears the child's "Now I lay me down to sleep." He hears
"the fortissimo of brazen bands" in the Mardi Gras parade as
well as the salvo of artillery on all battlefields. He hears what
is whispered in the closet. He hears what is shouted from
the housetop! He that planted the ear can hear.

Pray to God these words:

> God, touch my ears that I may hear
> Above earth's din, Thy voice ring clear.

By the ears of Jesus, ever attentive to a publican's prayer,
ever keenly sensitized to a child's cry, ever sympathetic with a
demoniac's wail, ever open to a leper's appeal for cleansing,
ever attentive to a sinner's cry for forgiveness, I pray you,
I beg you, to let your ears be yielded to God as instruments
of righteousness.

Have the ear of the wise which seeketh knowledge:

> The heart of the prudent getteth knowledge; and the ear
> of the wise seeketh knowledge (Prov. 18:15).

Remember these words:

> Whoso stoppeth his ears at the cry of the poor, he also
> shall cry himself, but shall not be heard (Prov. 21:13).

Let this be said of you:

> Blessed are . . . your ears, for they hear (Matt. 13:16).

Not this:

> But they refused to hearken, and pulled away the shoulder,
> and stopped their ears, that they should not hear (Zech. 7:11).

Nor this:

And they shall turn away their ears from the truth, and shall be turned unto fables (II Tim. 4:4).

Comfort your hearts with these words:

O that thou hadst hearkened to my commandments! then had thy peace been as a river, and thy righteousness as the waves of the sea (Isa. 48:18).

And give ear to these words:

He that hath an ear, let him hear what the Spirit saith unto the churches; To him that overcometh will I give to eat of the tree of life, which is in the midst of the paradise of God" (Rev. 2:7).

Chapter Four

THE MOUTH OF THE HUMAN BODY

*Who hath made man's mouth . . . have not I, the Lord
. . . I will be with thy mouth* (Ex. 4:11, 12).
My mouth shall praise thee with joyful lips (Ps. 63:5).
*A fool's mouth is his destruction, and his lips are the
snare of his soul* (Prov. 18:7).
Be not rash with thy mouth (Eccl. 5:2).
With the mouth confession is made unto salvation
(Rom. 10:10).
*This people draweth nigh unto me with their mouth,
and honoureth me with their lips; but their heart is far
from me* (Matt. 15:8).
*Set a watch, O Lord, before my mouth; keep the door
of my lips* (Ps. 141:3).

Think with me a moment of
THE CHRISTIAN'S BODY
1. It is *bought*.

Ye are bought with a price; be not ye the servants of men
(I Cor. 7:23).

For ye are bought with a price: therefore glorify God in your
body, and in your spirit, which are God's (I Cor. 6:20).

2. It is bought with a great *price*.

Forasmuch as ye know that ye were not redeemed with
corruptible things, as silver and gold, from your vain con-
versation received by tradition from your fathers; but with the
precious blood of Christ, as of a lamb without blemish and
without spot (I Pet. 1:18-19).

3. Being bought with a great price by another, it is *not your
own*.

What? know ye not that your body is the temple of the

55

Holy Ghost which is in you, which ye have of God, and ye
are not your own? (I Cor. 6:19)

4. It is the temple of the *Holy Spirit*.

Know ye not that ye are the temple of God, and that the
Spirit of God dwelleth in you? If any man defile the temple
of God, him shall God destroy; for the temple of God is holy,
which temple ye are (I Cor. 3:16-17).

5. It is to *glorify God*.

For ye are bought with a price: therefore glorify God in your
body, and in your spirit, which are God's (I Cor. 6:20).

6. It is for *the Lord* and the Lord is for *the body*.

Meats for the belly, and the belly for meats: but God shall
destroy both it and them. Now the body is not for fornication,
but for the Lord; and the Lord for the body (I Cor. 6:13).

7. It is to magnify *Christ*.

According to my earnest expectation and my hope, that in
nothing I shall be ashamed, but that with all boldness, as always, so now also Christ shall be magnified in my body, whether
it be by life, or by death (Phil. 1:20).

8. It is to *manifest* the life of Christ.

Always bearing about in the body the dying of the Lord Jesus,
that the life also of Jesus might be made manifest in our body
(II Cor. 4:10).

9. It is to be *controlled*.

But I keep under my body, and bring it into subjection: lest
that by any means, when I have preached to others, I myself
should be a castaway (I Cor. 9:27).

10. It is to be dissolved in *death* — if Jesus come not before
death makes dark visitation.

For we know that if our earthly house of this tabernacle
were dissolved, we have a building of God, an house not made
with hands, eternal in the heavens (II Cor. 5:1).

In the sweat of thy face shalt thou eat bread, till thou
return unto the ground; for out of it wast thou taken: for dust
thou art, and unto dust shalt thou return (Gen. 3:19).

11. It is to be *changed* when Christ comes.

Behold I shew you a mystery: We shall not all sleep, but we
shall all be changed, in a moment, in the twinkling of an eye,
at the last trump: for the trumpet shall sound, and the dead

shall be raised incorruptible, and we shall be changed (I Cor. 15:51-52).

Now in speaking on the mouth, I make one omission. I make no mention, or little mention, of the tongue in this message, even though some things said will make you think of the tongue. Today I would be as one who points to the pansy bed without mentioning the viper hidden therein. I would mention a palace of flesh and ivory and bone without asking you to look on the tiger enclosed. Making mention of the mouth and its usages without mention of the tongue is as one who speaks of a bunch of ripened bananas without taking note of the tarantula which abides in it, as one who looketh at a case of silver without noticing the sharp razor therein hidden.

In the Bible we find

MANY MENTIONS OF THE WORD MOUTH

The *dove's* mouth. The dove Noah sent out returned — "and, lo, in her mouth was an olive leaf" (Gen. 8:11).

The *well's* mouth. Jacob saw a well in the field — "and a great stone was upon the well's mouth" (Gen. 39:2).

The *sack's* mouth. When Joseph's brethren were returning from Egypt, their asses laded with corn, "as one of them opened his sack to give his ass provender in the inn, he espied his money . . . in his sack's mouth" (Gen. 42:27).

The *earth's* mouth. When, under the rebellion started by Korah, Dathan and Abiram, some "gathered themselves together against Moses and against Aaron. . . . the earth opened her mouth, and swallowed them up" (Num. 16:3, 32).

The *cave's* mouth. When Joshua found the five kings who hid themselves in a cave at Makkadah, he said, "Roll great stones upon the mouth of the cave" (Josh. 10:18).

The *lion's* mouth. David prayed: "Save me from the lion's mouth" (Ps. 22:21).

The *mule's* mouth. David advised: "Be ye not as . . . the

mule . . . whose mouth must be held in with bit and bridle" (Ps. 32:9).

The *pit's* mouth. David prayed: "Let not the pit shut her mouth upon me" (Ps. 69:15).

The *grave's* mouth. David, praying that his suit may be acceptable unto God, says: "Our bones are scattered at the grave's mouth, as when one cutteth and cleaveth wood" (Ps. 141:7).

The *furnace's* mouth. After Shadrach, Meshach and Abednego, servants of the most high God, were put in the fiery furnace, "then Nebuchadnezzar came near the the mouth of the burning fiery furnace" (Dan. 3:26).

The *den's* mouth. When Daniel was cast into the den of lions, "a stone was brought, and laid upon the mouth of the den" (Dan. 6:17).

But Daniel's testimony was: "My God . . . hath shut the lion's mouths" (Dan. 6:22).

The *bear's* mouth. In Daniel's vision of the four beasts, he saw a bear with three ribs in the mouth between the teeth of it (Dan. 7:5).

The *serpent's* mouth. We read of the dragon in the Book of Revelation this: "And the serpent cast out of his mouth water as a flood after the woman" (Rev. 12:15).

But today we speak of the *human* mouth — with truths that pertain thereunto.

Considering the mouth we think of

The Teeth of the Mouth

The body, an organism composed of thirty billion cells of various kinds, living bits of protoplasm, must convert food and air into energy and tissue. As the physiologist tells us, the food must be changed in such a way that it can be absorbed and carried to the different tissues. This is nothing more or less than the process of digestion. Speaking of this, Dr. Arthur

I. Brown says: "At the same time, air must enter the body, because there can be no combustion without oxygen. This is the process of respiration. After the altered food and air enter the body, they must be dissolved in some liquid medium. This medium is the blood. Then this liquid blood, filled with its supply of food for hungry cells, must be carried to all parts of the body in a steady and slow-moving stream. Here is where the pump and its thousands of miles of pipes are needed, the heart and the blood vessels having to do with the circulation, and making nutrition or metabolism possible. In the process of fuel combustion and conversion of food and air, there will be certain waste products — the ashes in the furnace."

But if our food is to be worked over by various chemicals in solution, this is done more effectively if the food is separated into the smallest possible portions. Meaning what? Meaning it must have a mill to grind it. This mill God has provided in the beautiful set of teeth — twenty in children and thirty-two in adults — ivory miniature mill stones — grinding, tearing, cutting instruments. Wonderful job these ivory mill stones do — if kept in condition and given time to do their work.

Now, as we have read, the work of teeth on food is wholly mechanical, even though the chemical part of digestion begins also in the mouth through the action of a fluid, saliva, secreted by three sets of glands. How marvelous the mouth with its roof and tongue and teeth!

But some spiritual lessons would we learn from the teeth. The teeth of the mouth teach us spiritual truths, such as: (1) *God's value of a little thing.*

> And if he smite out his manservant's tooth, or his maid-servant's tooth; he shall let him go free for his tooth's sake (Ex. 21:27).

The loss of one tooth meant that no more should a man be property in human flesh, that no more should he have no will but the will of his master, that no more should the slave master's whip be upon his back. The loss of one tooth meant all the years of his life should be years of liberty.

(2) *The reality and might of heredity.* Though God reproves the unjust proverb about the fathers eating sour grapes and the children's teeth being set on edge (Ezek. 18:2), and says that "every one shall die for his own iniquity" (Jer. 31:30), and there shall be a quickened sense of personal responsibility, still we see enough in these words to give us some thoughts on the truth of heredity—that a man can live so righteously as to bring blessings upon posterity, or he can sow such seed as to bring upon his children successive harvests of evil. Paul speaks of reaping the carnal things of others (I Cor. 9:11).

(3) *The bother the lazy man causes.*
As vinegar to the teeth, and as smoke to the eyes, so is the sluggard to them that send him (Prov. 10:26).
Josh Billings said: "Laziness is a good deal like money—the more a man has of it, the more he seems to want." How sad when any Christian is likened to a ship in the doldrums, likened unto "Joe the Marine who was so lazy he laid down his gun to sneeze."

(4) *The wounds made by an unfaithful person.*
Confidence in an unfaithful man in time of trouble is like a broken tooth, and a foot out of joint (Prov. 25:19).

(5) *The terror-producing fact of an awful hell.*
There shall be weeping and gnashing of teeth, when ye shall see Abraham, and Isaac, and Jacob, and all the prophets, in the kingdom of God, and you yourselves thrust out (Luke 13:28).

(6) *The rage of hatred.*
He teareth me in his wrath, who hateth me; he gnashed upon me with his teeth; mine enemy sharpeneth his eyes upon me (Job 16:9).

The wicked plotteth against the just, and gnashed upon him with his teeth (Ps. 37:12).

All thine enemies have opened their mouth against thee: they hiss and gnash the teeth: they say, We have swallowed her up: certainly this is the day that we looked for; we have found, we have seen it (Lam. 2:16).

When they heard these things, they were cut to the heart, and they gnashed on him with their teeth (Acts 7:54).

And now we consider:

THE LIPS OF THE MOUTH

The lips are called "the upper and nether part of the mouth." The lips are doors of flesh and muscle to keep in that which should not go out. And this the lips will do it they are yielded to God as instruments of righteousness.

Dirty words will not pass the doors of the lips. Paul says:

Let no corrupt communication proceed out of your mouth, but that which is good to the use of edifying, that it may minister grace unto the hearers (Eph.4:29).

A mouth yielded to God will not be "full of cursing and bitterness" (Rom. 3:14). There will be no denial by the mouth of "those things which God before had showed by the mouth of all his prophets" (Acts 3:18), no mouths opened "in blasphemy against God, to blaspheme his name, his tabernacle, and them that dwell in heaven" (Rev. 13:6); no mouths filled with senseless arguments (Job 23:4); no arrogancy coming out (I Sam. 2:3).

It is a dread omen of spiritual famine and national degeneration when many let corrupt communications proceed out of their mouths.

Lips yielded to God as instruments of righteousness will not be lips that shoot out in scorn (Ps. 22:7), nor lying lips which are an abomination to the Lord, nor a fool's lips entering into contention, nor lips that talk of mischief, nor lips that are a snare to one's own soul, nor lips that flatter, nor lips that are perverse. But yielded to God as instruments

of righteousness, the lips will be lips of truth to be established,
the lips of the righteous speaking things acceptable unto God,
the lips of knowledge which are as precious jewels, lips like
lilies dropping myrrh, lips that speak no guile, lips in which
God is glorified, lips that praise God.

We need to be wise in the matter of using the lips in
kissing, remembering that the kisses of pure love are like grains
of gold or silver found upon the ground, of no value themselves but precious as showing that a mine is near.

Byron said: "Eden revives in the first kiss of pure love."
Shakespeare said: "His kiss is as full of sanctity as the touch
of holy bread." Tennyson said: "Our souls rushed together at
the touching of the lips." Browning wrote:

> All the breath and the bloom of the year
>   in the bag of one bee;
> All the wonder and wealth of the mine in
>   the heart of one gem;
> And the core of one pearl all the shade and
>   shine of the sea;
> Breath and bloom, shade and shine, wonder,
>   wealth, and — how far above them —
> Truth that's brighter than gem,
> Truth that's purer than pearl, —
> Brightest truth, purest trust in the universe —
>   all were for me
> In the kiss of one girl!

Let us yield our lips to God so that they shall never kiss
deceitfully as Jacob kissed Isaac.

Let us never act toward Christ as did Judas who planted
treacherous kisses upon the cheek of Jesus.

But rather let our lips be "sweet lips whereon perpetually
remain the summer calm of golden charity," lips showing
forth loyalty as set forth in the words of John Charles McNeil:

> They put him in a prison cell
>   Murky and mean.
> She kissed him there a wife's farewell
>   The bars between.

And when she turned to go, the crowd,
Thinking to see her crushed and bowed,
Saw her pass out as proud
As any queen.

Let us beware that we give not nor receive the kisses of deceit. Solomon warns of the danger of giving welcome or acquiescence to the woman who "lieth in wait at every corner," kissing men with an impudent face. And Maeterlinck says: "Had your eyes been opened, you would have perceived in a kiss what now you behold in catastrophe."

Yield, you young people whom I love and for whom I would die, your lips to God as instruments of righteousness. Then your love affairs will not be as plentiful as blackberries. Then there will not be promiscuous kissing, kissing whereby you play at love-making and make love lose its sacredness. Such careless use of the lips makes caresses become cheap and common things, dispensed to almost any passerby. A girl who so unguardedly yields her lips, to use a figure from James Lane Allen, becomes like a bunch of grapes above a common path where everyone that passes takes a grape. He who takes does so without reverence and to his own impoverishment. It is impossible to sow your affections broadcast and keep them in wise reserve at the same time. You cannot keep the water cool and use up the ice. You cannot keep the coffee hot and dispense with fire or throw the thermos bottle away.

Thus it happens that many a young man and many a young woman squander so much in petty flirtations that when they come to the supreme moment of life they have made themselves incapable of a really great love. In the golden coin of real and abiding affection, such spendthrifts soon become utter bankrupts. Sometimes, too, this self-squandering goes further than mere flirtations. It goes even to positive shame. How young people need to pray: "Keep the door of my lips."

But lips yielded to God as instruments of righteousness will be doors to keep out what ought not to go in the mouth and into the stomach. Lips that are instruments of righteousness will keep out all forms of strong drink.

The Bible says:

> Wine is a mocker, strong drink is raging: and whosoever is deceived thereby is not wise (Prov. 20:1).
>
> Who hath woe? who hath sorrow? who hath contentions? who hath babbling? who hath wounds without cause? who hath redness of eyes? They that tarry long at the wine, they that go to seek mixed wine. Look not thou upon the wine when it is red, when it giveth his colour in the cup, when it moveth itself aright. At the last it biteth like a serpent, and stingeth like an adder (Prov. 23:29-32).

All that people say in favor of intoxicating liquor is as worthless for purchase as counterfeit money, as worthless as painted water for the thirsty. And I can say better things about the rattlesnake and the skunk than I can about liquor — legal or illegal. You can search through all histories, delve into all philosophies, look into all tombs, walk through all mad houses, listen to all testimonies, and you can not find one good thing that can be said about the open traffic in liquor. "With its breath of poison it has wiped whole nations from the face of the earth. It has caused men to discard honor. It has caused women to discard virtue. It has filled insane asylums and prisons. It has stolen sons and daughters from fathers and mothers. With one touch it has ruined great industries. It has burned cities. It has sunk navies and destroyed armies. It has turned gold into dross, health into misery, beauty into caricature, and pride to shame. Of character, it is the coral reef on which the ship goes down. Of life, it is rust that consumes. Of the citadel of the soul, it is the traitor that lets the enemy in."

Intoxicating beverages never touched an individual that it did not leave upon him an indelible stain. It never touched a family that it did not plant the seeds of misery and dissolution. It never touched a community that it did not lower the moral tone, chill religion and undermine law. It never touched a state that it did not multiply crime, destroy wealth and increase the burdens of taxation. It never touched a nation that it did not clog the machinery of government, blight prosperity, weaken patriotism, and encourage treason.

No one can claim to have lips of righteousness who permits to pass through them alcoholic beverage, which is a narcotic poison, which dulls the nerves and takes the water out of every tissue with which it comes in contact. It dries the throat, causing the desire for another drink. It irritates the lining of the stomach, finally causing ulcers. It lessens the efficiency of every organ of the body and blunts the moral sense.

Strong drink debases.

> But they also have erred through wine, and strong drink are out of the way; the priest and the prophet have erred through strong drink, they are swallowed up of wine, they are out of the way through strong drink; they err in vision, they stumble in judgment. For all tables are full of vomit and filthiness, so that there is no place clean (Is. 28:7-8).

Strong drink leads to licentiousness.

> Look not thou upon the wine when it is red, when it giveth his colour in the cup, when it moveth itself aright. At the last it biteth like a serpent, and stingeth like an adder (Prov. 23: 31-33).

"At the last": there is a day of reckoning, when the will is finally yielded and the individual wholly surrendered to the habit, given over to wounds and woes, to sorrow of soul and body, seeing no harm in indulgence and no benefit in abstinence.

Strong drink leads men's hearts from God.

> And the harp, and the viol, the tabret, and the pipe, and wine, are in their feasts: but they regard not the work of the Lord, neither consider the operation of his hands. Therefore my people are gone into captivity, because they have no knowledge: and their honourable men are famished, and their multitude dried up with thirst. Therefore hell hath enlarged herself, and opened her

mouth without measure: and their glory, and their multitude, and their pomp, and he that rejoiceth, shall descend into it (Is. 5: 12-14).

But give thought to the

Voice of the Mouth

Remarkable and distinguishing are the capacities and functions of the human voice. Some people have spoken disparagingly of the human voice in words like these:

A voice like a broken phonograph.
Her voice was like a bagpipe suffering from tonsilitis.
A voice like a concertina that has been left out in the rain.
A voice like the cry of an expiring mouse, shrill and thin.
Gruff voice, like the creaking of the gallows chain.
A voice like a strained foghorn.
A voice like a coyote with bronchitis.
A voice like the voice of a frog with quinsy.
A voice like dishwater gurgling through a sink.

Some have spoken in praise of the voice:

Thy voice like an echo from Fairyland seems.
Her voice is like the harmony of angels.
It was a voice so mellow, so bright and warm and round,
As if a beam of sunshine had been melted into sound.
A voice like the music of rills.
Her voice is like the evening thrush
That sings in Cessnook banks unseen,
While his mate sits nestling in the bush.
A voice as sweet as the evening breeze of Boreas in the
pleasant month of November.
Delicate voices like silver bells.
A voice soft with solitudes.

And the Bible speaks of the voice of blood, of weeping, of shouting, of "the still small voice after the fire," of the roaring voice, the voice of thunder, the voice of thanksgiving, and the voice of supplications.

We read in the Bible of the voice of the floods, the voice of a psalm, the voice of joy, the voice of groaning, of understanding, the voice of the truth, the voice of a woman in travail, the

voice of doves, the voice out of the cloud, the voice of God —
and many other voices signifying the use of the mouth.

Remarkable and distinguishing are the marvelous mechan-
isms of the human body. But no less remarkable and distinguishing are the capacities and functions of the human voice.
Somewhere I read this tribute to the human voice: "It is as
diverse from all other voices as if it had been intended for a
different world — as, no doubt, it was. For variety of sounds
and power of expression it can be compared with any other
only in the way of contrast. In music, it so far surpasses any
other voice, or any instrument that none can be named in
connection with it. From the lowest gutteral bass to the
trill of highest pitch it sweeps the whole range of melodies with
a sweetness, an expression and a pathos, all its own. It is the
most perfect vehicle of emotion. Every different sensibility
of the human body has its peculiar tone. Grief and joy, love
and hatred, compassion and revenge, humility and pride, may
each express itself perfectly by the tone, without a spoken
word, and each expresses the degree of its intensity. Its power
of varied articulation is inconceivable — for aught I know it
may be infinite — so flexible, so perfect is the vocal apparatus.

"Take all possible vowel, and consonant, and guttural
sounds, and in all their possible combinations, and all variations
of tone, and inflection, and emphasis, in which they may be
uttered, with every shade of difference in swell and cadence,
in force, in melody, and in every conceivable particular of
variety and difference, in every respect, and you shall find that
human speech, considered in its merely physical aspects, might
furnish matter of study for a lifetime. Hear it in the whisper,
the common tone, the call, the outcry, the shout, the shriek.
Hear it stating facts, explaining, arguing, insisting, exhorting,
beseeching, pleading, wooing, cooing, coaxing, chuckling,
exulting, laughing, expostulating, warning, affirming, denying,

scolding, reproving, commanding, rebuking, condemning, approving, commending, complimenting, criticising, carping, cajoling, bantering, complaining, correcting — with an adapted tone for every various purpose of speech. How every tone affects you — pleases you, vexes you, enraptures you, rouses you, wins you!" How important that the mouth, because of the voice, be yielded to God as an instrument of righteousness.

Now let us think of the enrichment that will come to us and of how God will be glorified because of the mouth if we have the

Righteous Mouth

I mean by this that we yield our mouths to God as instruments of righteousness. Then our own mouths will not condemn us. Then we can say what Hannah said:

> And Hannah prayed, and said, My heart rejoiceth in the Lord, mine horn is exalted in the Lord: my mouth is enlarged over mine enemies; because I rejoice in thy salvation (I Sam. 2:1).

Then, as to those in sorrow, we can say what Job said to his miserable comforters:

> But I would strengthen you with my mouth, and the moving of my lips should assuage your grief (Job 16:5).

Then we will purpose what David purposed:

> Thou hast proved mine heart; thou hast visited me in the night; thou hast tried me, and shalt find nothing; I am purposed that my mouth shall not transgress (Ps. 17:3).

Then we will be able to testify what the Psalmist testified:

> I will bless the Lord at all times: his praise shall continually be in my mouth (Ps. 34:1).

> Let the words of my mouth, and the meditation of my heart, be acceptable in thy sight, O Lord, my strength and my redeemer (Ps. 19:14).

Then, knowing the danger of a runaway mouth, we will make determination to make it honor God, saying:

> I will take heed to my ways, that I sin not with my tongue:

I will keep my mouth with a bridle, while the wicked is before me (Ps. 39:1).

Then, as we think upon the goodness of God, we will say:
I will greatly praise the Lord with my mouth; yea, I will praise him among the multitude (Ps. 109:30).
My mouth shall speak the praise of the Lord: and let all flesh bless his holy name for ever and ever (Ps. 145:21).

Then, desiring truth in the inward parts, we shall pray:
And take not the word of truth utterly out of my mouth; for I have hoped in thy judgments (Ps. 119:43).

Then, in speaking against evils, we will have the experience and testimony set forth by Isaiah:
And he hath made my mouth like a sharp sword (Is. 49:2).

Then, glorifying God in our bodies, we shall not "be rash with our mouths to utter perverse things," and no arrogancy shall come out of our mouths, and the law of truth will be in our mouths.

And in yielding our mouths to God as instruments of righteousness our inspiration shall be the

MOUTH AND BODY OF JESUS

His human body was a real body. Those were real feet drenched by the tears of the penitent woman; that was a real head that the devoted Mary anointed aforehand for the burial; those were real hands which the nails fastened to the beams of the Cross; those were real eyes that suffered with sympathy at the tomb of Lazarus; that was no phantom cheek which Judas kissed; it was a real side which the spear of the Roman soldier cleft; and a real broken heart from whence blood and water flowed. That was a real dead body, limp and helpless with that strange helplessness and weightiness which death causes, that was taken down from the Cross, wrapped in cerements and laid in Joseph's new tomb. Touch Him anywhere and you elicit the traits and responses of humanity.

Consider, sir!
A human heart beat there! a human brain
Pondered and pitied and was sorrowful,
Behind that soverign brow. The blood of us —
Of women and of men — coursed crimson, warm,
In those rich veins! Nay, and He ate our meats
And drank our drinks, and wore the dress we wore;
And His hair fluttered in the breeze which stirred
Peter's and John's and mine.

Of his holy mouth the Bible speaks:

But with righteousness shall he judge the poor, and reprove with equity for the meek of the earth and he shall smite the earth with the rod of his mouth, and with the breath of his lips shall he slay the wicked (Is. 11:-).

Let him kiss me with the kisses of his mouth (S. of Sol. 1:2).

His mouth is most sweet: yea, he is altogether lovely. This is my beloved, and this is my friend, O daughters of Jerusalem (S. of Sol. 5:16).

Neither was any deceit in his mouth (Is. 53:9).

Who did no sin, neither was guile found in his mouth (I Peter 2:22).

In the synagogue in Nazareth "there was delivered unto him the book of the prophet Esaias." Then opening the book, He read.

And he closed the book, and he gave it again to the minister, and sat down. And the eyes of all them that were in the synagogue were fastened on him. And he began to say unto them, This day is the scripture fulfilled in your ears. And all bare him witness, and wondered at the gracious words which proceeded out of his mouth (Luke 4:20-22).

Paul, speaking of his conversion, said

And one Ananias, a devout man according to the law, having a good report of all the Jews which dwelt there, came unto me, and stood, and said unto me, Brother Saul, receive thy sight. And the same hour I looked up upon him. And he said, The God of our fathers hath chosen thee, that thou shouldest know his will, and see that Just One, and shouldest hear the voice of his mouth (Acts 22:12-14).

Writing to the Thessalonians, Paul said:

> For the mystery of iniquity doth already work: only he who
> now letteth will let, until he be taken out of the way. And
> then shall that Wicked be revealed, whom the Lord shall con-
> sume with the spirit of his mouth, and shall destroy with the
> brightness of his coming (II Thess. 2:7-8).

And John, with revelation from Jesus himself as he was
in the midst of the golden candlesticks, wrote:

> So then because thou art lukewarm, and neither cold nor hot,
> I will spue thee out of my mouth (Rev. 3:16).

So I beg you by the mouth of Jesus in which there is no
deceit, from which gracious words proceeded, let your ears
receive the words of His mouth and yield your mouths to
God as instruments of righteousness.

And despise not the words of His mouth as did those who
"filled a sponge with vinegar and gall and put it to his mouth."
By His mouth into which hunger came and in which thirst
dwelt, I pray that you will let no corrupt communication
proceed out of your mouth and no evil thing enter into your
mouth.

And forget not this — as we look at Him upon the Cross:

> And when they had platted a crown of thorns, they put it
> upon his head, and a reed in his right hand: and they bowed
> the knee before him, and mocked him, saying, Hail, King of
> the Jews! (Matt. 27:29).
>
> Let Christ the King of Israel descend now from the cross,
> that we may see and believe. And they that were crucified with
> him reviled him (Mark 15:32).
>
> Who did no sin, neither was guile found in his mouth:
> who, when he was reviled, reviled not again; when he suffered,
> he threatened not; but committed himself to him that judgeth
> righteously: who his own self bare our sins in his own body on
> the tree, that we, being dead to sins, should live unto righteous-
> ness: by whose stripes ye were healed (I Peter 2:22-24).

And you who are criticized by friends or by foes, receive
unto your hearts these words:

And he made his grave with wicked, and with the rich in his death; because he had done no violence, neither was any deceit in his mouth (Is. 53:9).

He was oppressed, and he was afflicted, yet he opened not his mouth (Isa. 53:7).

Chapter Five

THE TONGUE OF THE HUMAN BODY

For in many things we offend all. If any man offend not in word, the same is a perfect man, and able also to bridle the whole body (Jas. 3:2).

If any man among you seem to be religious, and bridleth not his tongue, but deceiveth his own heart, this man's religion is vain (Jas. 1:26).

Death and life are in the power of the tongue: and they that love it shall eat the fruit thereof (Prov. 18:21).

When we read the Bible — Book above and beyond all books as a river is beyond a rill in reach, Book beyond all books as the sun is beyond a tallow dip in brightness — we find that in commanding the obedience of mankind, it speaks much of the human body and its members. And not a few words but many words do we read within its sacred pages of the tongue. Lines wherein mention of the tongue and its usages are found are as plentiful as flowers in a spring garden, as various in description of the tongue as fishes found in seven seas, as strong as the devils in the Gadarene demoniac. Yes, often is the tongue the topic of the Bible—that Book which is divine in authorship, human in penmanship, universal in scope, infallible in authority, validated and confirmed by the Holy Spirit with a divine certainty that is incommunicable by reason and impervious to the assaults of doubt, the miracle book of diversity in unity. While some topics are dealt with in comprehensive brevity, the loose tongue has a whole chapter given to it in the Epistle of James.

The human tongue is made up of many muscles turning and intertwining astonishingly. Paley writes: "It is worth any man's while to watch the agility of his tongue; the wonderful promptitude with which it executes change of position, and the perfect exactness. Each syllable of articulated sound requires for its utterance a specific action of the tongue, and of the parts adjacent to it. The disposition and configuration of the mouth for every letter and word is not only peculiar, but if nicely and accurately attended to, perceptible to the sight! . . . How instantaneously are these positions assumed and dismissed! How numerous are the permutations, how various, yet how infallible!"

Unless the tongue be yielded to God as an instrument of righteousness, it will be a

TERRIBLE TONGUE

The terror of an unrighteous tongue is shown in strikingly descriptive Biblical words, is shown by the indictment passed upon the tongue by sacred writers. Note:

> The tongue is a fire.
> The tongue is full of deadly poison.
> The tongue is a little member ⌈of the body⌉ and boasteth great things.
> The tongue an unruly evil.
> The tongue is a world of iniquity.
> The tongue defileth the whole body.
> The tongue setteth on fire the course of nature.
> The tongue can no man tame.

Job spoke of the tongue as a *scourge*.

> Thou shalt be hid from the scourge of the tongue: neither shalt thou be afraid of destruction when it cometh (Job 5:21).

The Psalmist indicted the tongue as an instrument of unrighteousness in these words:

> For there is no faithfulness in their mouth; their inward part is very wickedness; their throat is an open sepulchre; they flatter with their tongue (Ps. 5:9).

> The Lord shall cut off all flattering lips, and the tongue that speaketh proud things (Ps. 12:3).

The Apostle Peter, recalling some Old Testament wisdom, wrote:

> For he that will love life, and see good days, let him refrain his tongue from evil, and his lips that they speak no guile (I Peter 3:10).

The terror of an unrighteous tongue is set forth in words closely akin — written by the Psalmist and the author of Proverbs:

> Thy tongue deviseth mischiefs; like a sharp razor, working deceitfully (Ps. 52:2).
> There is that speaketh like the piercings of a sword (Prov. 12:18).

And God in His holy hatred of evil finds equally guilty the liar's devilish tongue and the murderer's bloody hands.

> A proud look, a lying tongue, and hands that shed innocent blood (Prov. 6:17).
> Death and life are in the power of the tongue (Prov. 18:21).

The tongue is a trouble producer for the soul. This is shown in these words:

> Whoso keepeth his mouth and his tongue keepeth his soul from troubles (Prov. 21:23).

Paul, in the third chapter of Romans, is as a prosecutor giving a summary against man. Out of six counts having to do with man's body, four implicate and indict the tongue:

> Their throat is an open sepulchre; with their tongues they have used deceit; the poison of asps is under their lips: whose mouth is full of cursing and bitterness (Rom. 3:13, 14).

The terror of the unruly tongue is set forth in these words — sober words which we should seriously and penitently, with humility and humiliation, ponder:

> His mouth is full of cursing and deceit and fraud: under his tongue is mischief and vanity (Ps. 10:7).
> The Lord shall cut off all flattering lips, and the tongue that speaketh proud things (Ps. 12:3).

And how great is God's goodness shown in these words: "Thou shalt keep them . . . from the strife of tongues" (Ps. 31:20).

What a terror the tongue is when it transgresses the laws of God for the tongue. How we need to pray that God will keep our tongues from evil and our lips from speaking guile.

Now let us think of the

TORMENTING TONGUE

There are many things that torment us. The filthy fly, carrying disease, making the butter the landing place for his dirty feet or the glass of milk his swimming pool — and finding no place to land, when we seek sleep, except the tip of the nose or the bald place on our heads — is a great tormentor.

The rat, purveyor of plague, gnawing annoyingly in the still hours of the night, robbing us of sleep and destroying valuable treasures and using the velvet of the piano for the making of his bed, is a sly tormentor.

The drip of the leaky water faucet — "oft in the stilly night" — dropping our comfort into the chasm of its irritable persistence, is a tormentor indeed.

The bed bug, despicable in the way he makes his living, impudent in his uncultered invasion into our bed areas, together with the pillows thereof, is a great tormentor.

An aching tooth, pounding every nerve with the invisible fists of pain, is a tormentor indeed. The aching ear, acting as though it would fain remove its habitation from the head, gives torment which is not to be desired.

Cigarette smoke, blown north, south, east, west by those who care not whom it irritates, is, to all hay fever victims, a tormentor indeed.

The mosquito, with a solo flight that holds a hum that harasses like the whine of a Scotch bagpipe, as alien to melody as poison to health, filling his maw with man's blood and then, in base ingratitude, giving him a hypodermic of malaria, is a tormentor indeed. Writing of the malicious mosquito,

someone has said that the rattlesnake strikes to defend himself, the skunk will not distribute his perfumery unless he
is in danger, the lions kill for food, hunger and its young
governs the predatory eagle, the fox robs the hen roost because he has a stomach to feed, even man — the most re-
lentless and successful in sin and wrong — kills cattle for provender and to get leather for his shoes, and shoots quail
ostensibly to adorn his table. The tornado may be the only
way of restoring the equilibrium of the air, the volcanic erup-
tion may be due to some sort of terrestrial indigestion (judging
from the sulphuric belches it emits); but the mosquito makes
us think of the purely malicious in life.

Then this same writer (I am sorry I cannot remember his
name) says that it appears to be the unavoidable truth that
some folks are just plain mean. In children we sometimes
see it, because even the most angelic of them take pleasure at
times in causing pain. Most of them happily get over this.
Some do not. Some men take pleasure in tormenting their
wives. Some folks are so full of petty spite that they go out
of their way to do some one an evil turn. Some thugs there
are who beat men for the pleasure of the exercise. Some
teamsters there are who lash horses to see them suffer. Some
boys there are who torment cats to hear their cries of agony.
Some pranksters there are who tie strings across side walks
and laugh to see people stumble and fall. Some people there
are who like to put flies in someone's ointment.

People who say there is no personal devil should explain
about the someone or the somewhat that gets into men and
women and dehumanizes them — makes them hurt people
and have little regret as to wounds made. What tormentors are
people whose tongues know no more about putting down a
period than a monkey knows about trigonometry! What tormentors can people be whose talkative tongues find no more
rest than "old man river who jes' keeps rollin' along" — no

more rest than the rasping jaws of the mouse disturbing more than occasional thunder. Surely there is no torment so ruinous, so mean, so malicious as the torment of the tongue which never observes the law of kindness.

I think Joseph was tormented more by the lying tongue of Potiphar's wife than by the depths of the dungeon and the jail bars. I am sure Moses was tormented more by the murmuring and complaining of the people than by the plagues of frogs and flies and lice and boils and blain and blood in Egypt, because we read:

> And they said unto Moses, because there were no graves in Egypt, hast thou taken us away to die in the wilderness? wherefore hast thou dealt thus with us, to carry us forth out of Egypt? (Ex. 14:11).
>
> And the whole congregation of the children of Israel murmured against Moses and Aaron in the wilderness: and the children of Israel said unto them, Would to God we had died by the hand of the Lord in the land of Egypt, when we sat by the flesh pots, and when we did eat bread to the full; for ye have brought us forth into this wilderness, to kill this whole assembly with hunger (Ex. 16:2-3).
>
> And the people thirsted there for water; and the people murmured against Moses, and said, Wherefore is this that thou hast brought us up out of Egypt, to kill us and our children and our cattle with thirst? (Ex. 17:3).

More tormenting to Moses than the hardships of the wilderness wanderings were the tongues of Miriam and Aaron who spoke "against Moses because of the Ethiopian woman whom he had married" (Num. 12:1). When God's anger was kindled against the seditious two, then God asked, "Wherefore then were ye not afraid to speak against my servant Moses?" — and then "Miriam became leprous, white as snow."

More tormenting to Samson than the young lion who met him out of the vineyards of Timnath, the lion which "he rent as he would have rent a kid," was the tongue of Samson's wife, who wept before him, saying, "Thou dost but hate me, and lovest me not: thou hast put forth a riddle unto the

children of my people, and hast not told me" (Judg. 14:16).
More tormenting than the Philistines to Samson was the
tongue of Delilah who sought to find wherein his great
strength lay:

> And she said unto him, How canst thou say, I love thee,
> when thine heart is not with me? thou hast mocked me these
> three times, and hast not told me wherein thy great strength
> lieth (Judg. 16:15).

More tormenting to David than Goliath's size and armor
was the tongue of Goliath, for 'tis written: "And the Philis-
tine cursed David by his gods" (I Sam. 17:43).

More tormenting to David than the stones cast at him
and at all the servants of King David by Shimei was the
cursing tongue of Shimei (II Sam. 16:6ff).

More tormenting to David than his hunger and thirst
and weariness in the wilderness was the tongue of Absalom
which stole the hearts of many from love and loyalty to the
King.

More tormenting to Jesus than the pangs of hunger was
the tongue of Satan in the wilderness, and the tongues
of those who falsely accused Him.

More tormenting, too, to Paul than the many stripes laid
on him in Philippi were the tongues of "certain philosophers of
the Epicureans, and of the Stoicks," who "encountered him.
And some said, what will this babbler say? . . . And when they
heard of the resurrection of the dead, some mocked" (Acts 17).

What a tormentor the tongue has been in the world. It has
been a dagger to stab the hearts of loved ones with its sharp
thrust of pain. It has been a scourge to torture the lives
of those who live nearest us. It has been a whetted sword. It
has been a mortar out of which has sped the bomb that has
exploded and rent asunder whole communities. It has been
a razor wielded as by a madman on a children's playground.
It has been a battering ram that drives its way through walls
of communities and breaks down society. It has been a

thunderbolt that crashes the organ with force into splinters and leaves it without shape or tone. It has been an instrument of giving all conceivable pain to men.

I read the other day that the Spanish in Cuba before the war between Spain and the United States were wont to put their pitiable Cuban victims to torture by pouring into the ear molten lead from the hot crucibles and thus give them excruciating pain. But how much more poignant anguish has been given by means of the tongue as it has poured into the ears of men the words red hot with malignant hatred and with ridicule and sacriligious sarcasm and with folly and shameful wrong. I think the tongue may be indicted as the worst criminal in the world with all the guilt of the Devil, since by blasphemy of God and by blasting human life with its devastating power, it is a satanic mischief.

Better, for the welfare of mankind, the tongue should be torpid as a toad in marble than the tormenting tongue which, like the dart of death, spares neither sex nor age.

But I would have us think now of the

TONGUE AS A TORCH

> Even so the tongue is a little member, and boasteth great things. Behold, how great a matter a little fire kindleth! And the tongue is a fire, a world of iniquity: so is the tongue among our members, that it defileth the whole body, and setteth on fire the course of nature; and is set on fire of hell (James 3:5-6).

How sobering these words! Hell has more to do in promoting the fire of the tongue than men believe. An uncontrolled tongue, set on fire of hell, is mischievous beyond words. It produces hatred, anger, rage, contentions and those evil things which serve the purpose of the Devil. We should dread the evils of the careless and evil tongue as we dread fire, because "a careless word may kindle strife; a cruel word may wreck a life; a bitter word may hate instill, a brutal word may smite and kill."

The tongue can be a fagot of hell. The tongue is as dangerous as fire when fire is the master. As a spark can set a forest on fire, as one little lighted match can start a conflagration in a city, so the tongue kindles the whole nature into flame.

Recently the Associated Press reported that an Air Force officer said that the atomic bomb is the size of a golf ball and is equal to 5,400,000 pounds of TNT. Lt. Col. William R. Stark, member of a five-man team from the Industrial College of the Armed Forces, puts it this way: "The atomic bomb, the size of one golf ball, would be the equivalent of 270 ten-ton TNT bombs. The damage of such a bomb comes from three sources — blast, flash heat and radioactivity." But the tongue, itself set on fire of hell, is more of a devilish torch than the atomic bomb.

> Sometimes Death chooses pestilence or flames,
>   Hot avalanches of the molten sand,
> Or lightning bolts hurled recklessly thro' space,
>   Or famine stalking hungrily the land.
>
> Sometimes titantic mounds of glacial ice
>   The instruments come to blot out life,
> The mighty earth may quiver — break apart,
>   Or nation slaughter nation in war's strife.
>
> A cloud of vapor, poisonous and rank,
>   Makes shrouds for thousands, checking life and breath.
> All these and more gigantic forces serve
>   As the command of the destroyer Death.
> But the warmest love may die perchance
>   From bitter word or hostile glance.

Thus we are made to think of the tongue, a deadly evil, which does more hurt than catastrophes of earth, because it "setteth on fire the whole course of nature."

Better, for mankind — for young, for old, for all — the talk-less tongue than the tongue which is a torch — like the incendiary's flambeau.

Better — for others — for folks to be "speechless as a mummy" than to have tongues such as Joseph Hale spoke of who said: "His tongue, like the tails of Samson's foxes, carried firebrands, and is enough to set the whole field of the world on a flame."

I think, too, I prefer the mouth that has a speechless tongue to the mouth with a tongue thus described: "His tongue is like a Bagpipe Drone, that has no Stop, but makes a continual noise, as long as he can squeeze any wind out of himself."

"If any man offend not in word, the same is a perfect man, and able also to bridle the whole body." (James 3:2)

But think with me of the

TRADUCING TONGUE

To traduce means to misrepresent willfully the character or conduct of someone. It means to defame, to slander, to calumniate. Roger Williams said: "The weak and peaceable are traduced as rivals."

The traducing tongue is indeed "a world of iniquity." The tongue that slanders is a traducing tongue. It is like a hidden assassin who shoots his arrows in the dark. No wonder Plautus said: "Those who carry about, and those who listen to slander, should, if I could have my way, all be hanged — the tattlers by the tongue, the listeners by their ears."

> A wicked doer giveth heed to false lips; and a liar giveth ear to a naughty tongue (Prov. 17:4)
> He that hath a froward heart findeth no good: and he that hath a perverse tongue falleth into mischief (Prov. 17:20).

Tennyson said of Vivien, who contributed not a little to the breaking up of King Arthur's Round Table:

> She let her tongue
> Rage like a fire among the noblest names,
> Polluting and imputing the whole self,
> Defaming and defacing till she left
> Not even Lancelot brave nor Gallahad clean.

And Shakespeare said:

> 'Tis slander
> Whose edge is sharper than the sword; whose tongue
> Outvenoms all the worms of Nile, whose breath
> Rides on the posting winds, and doth belie
> All corners of the world; kings, queens and states,
> Maids, matrons — nay, the secrets of the grave
> This viperous slander enters.

The traducing tongue steals a good name which is rather to be chosen than great riches. A man's name is himself. To rob him of his good name is fundamentally to violate the eighth commandment. Truly did Shakespeare write:

> Who steals my purse, steals trash,
> But he who filches from me my good name
> Robs me of that which enriches not him
> And makes me poor indeed.

To traduce one's good name is like stealing bread from the hungry with no better purpose than to throw it in the sewer. The traducing tongue of slander and gossip is yet the cancer of the social body, the leprosy of the community, the pestilence that walketh at noonday, the destruction that wasteth at midnight, the hailstorm beating with icy hammers, the flood sweeping away sacred things, the fire that burns to ashes and the cold that freezes to the marrow.

A traducing tongue is an assassinator of character, a purveyor of moral poison, a viper that stings to death the reputation of others, a vulture that lives off the carrion of lies, a hyena that digs into the graves of the departed that it may drag forth the corpse of some wrong act, a scavenger that drives its cart through every community.

The traducing tongue is the climax of meanness, the apotheosis of the absurd, sackcloth at a wedding, bones at a banquet, sarcastic laughter at a funeral. And gossip, another product of the traducing tongue, is a humming bird with eagle wings and a voice like a foghorn. It can be heard from Dan to Beersheba, and has caused more trouble and heartache than the world will know until the universe shuts up and begins the final invoice.

George Meredith said: "Gossip is a beast of prey that does not wait for the death of the creature it devours."

In the words of another, "A bitter word dropped from our lips against a brother is like a pistol fired amongst mountains. The sharp report is caught up and intensified and echoed by rocks and caves, till it emulates the thunder. So a thoughtless, unkind word in passing from mouth to mouth receives progressive exaggerations, and, snowball-like, increases as it rolls."

Gossip mongers are persons who tear the bandages from social wounds, and prevent their healing; they are persons who bring flint and steel, and acid and alkali together, and are justly chargeable with all the fire and ebullition. A whispered word of slander is like that fox with a fire brand tied to its tail that Samson sent among the standing corn of the Philistines. A gossip in a village, or anywhere, is like a viper in a bed.

At the close of a talkative ladies aid session at which the ladies had over-indulged in gossiping comments about various members of the community, a young woman who had attended for the first time proceeded to call the group the "Ladies Raid Society." Nor would she stand correction. "Raid Society!" she exploded. "You have raided homes and good names and reputations plenty this afternoon. Good day!" The society at once underwent a radical change.

The lying tongue that traduces, God lists along with the most evil of evildoers:

> But the fearful, and unbelieving, and the abominable, and murderers, and whoremongers, and sorcerers, and idolaters, and all liars, shall have their part in the lake which burneth with fire and brimstone: which is the second death (Rev. 21:8).

The lying tongue has caused wars between nations, separations of husbands and wives, barriers between brothers and sisters, father and son, mother and daughter, friends and neighbors. Lying tongues have produced feuds that have lasted for decades, even centuries. Lying tongues have blackened the reputations of young girls, beardless boys, happy ambitious matrons who are rearing families, and old men whose lives are almost spent. Lying tongues have split churches, hindered Christian progress, and planted the germ of bitterness and hatred in the hearts of millions of people, and this germ has passed on from generation to generation. If all the tears that lying and unruly tongues have caused to be shed were put in one place, they would make a river. The traducing tongue has caused enough sighs to create the moan of a perpetual storm — and has been the source of enough misery and despondency to wipe every smile from every pair of human lips. Satanic the traducing tongue that is a trader in scandal and evil gossip.

I would think now of the

TAR TONGUE

I mean by that the tongue which, in several ways, gives people a coat of tar and feathers. The backbiter has a tongue of tar. In Psalm 15 the citizen of Zion is described as one who "backbiteth not with his tongue." He says nothing that might hurt his neighbor in his character, person, property. He is the author of no slander. He insinuates nothing by which his neighbor may be injured.

Dr. Adam Clarke said: "The word 'backbite' was intended to convey the treble sense of knavishness, cowardice and brutality. He is a knave who would rob you of your good name, a coward who would speak of you in your absence what he dared not do in your presence — and only an ill-conditioned dog would fly at and bite your back when your face was turned. Hence, the backbiter's tongue is the tongue of a knave, a coward, a dog."

Backbiters are classed in the Bible with an awful crowd. They are classed with those who do not like to retain God in their knowledge:

> Being filled with all unrighteousness, fornication, wickedness, covetousness, maliciousness; full of envy, murder, debate, deceit, malignity; whisperers, backbiters, haters of God, despiteful, proud, boasters, inventors of evil things, disobedient to parents, without understanding, covenantbreakers, without natural affection, implacable, unmerciful: who knowing the judgment of God, that they which commit such things are worthy of death, not only do the same but have pleasure in them that do them (Rom. 1:29-32).

The tongue that smears with tar is a talebearing tongue. The talebearer is a slanderer, a busybody; one who takes up a reproach against his neighbor and spreads it abroad. There is a "shalt not" with respect to this matter, and it is just as binding on us from the Divine point of view as "Thou shalt not kill.": "Thou shalt not go up and down as a talebearer among thy people" (Lev. 19:16). In the name of God and holy religion, let every one who reads these lines covenant with God, and with one another, that we will forever quit such business.

Well, you say, "But it is the truth; and the truth hurts no one." That may be true, but the repeating of it is *evil speaking* and God condemns evil speaking. The wisest of men, Solomon, has said in Proverbs:

> A talebearer revealeth secrets (11:13). He that covereth a transgression seeketh love; but he that repeateth a matter separateth very friends (17:9). The words of a talebearer are as wounds, and they go down into the innermost parts of the belly (18:8). He that goeth about as a talebearer revealeth secrets: therefore meddle not with him that flattereth with his lips (20:19). Where no wood is, there the fire goeth out: so where there is no talebearer, the strife ceaseth (26:20).

The tongue that spreads tar is a faultfinding tongue. It takes no brains to find fault. A buzzard can always find a carcass. A fly can always find a sore. A hog can always find a place to wallow. A butcher bird can always find a thorn or a spike on which to impale its victim. Tennyson spoke of those

> Who hate each other for a song,
> And do their little best to bite
> And pinch their brethren in the throng,
> And scratch the very dead for spite.

We tell, we are told. And mythology tells us that when Jupiter — years and years and years ago — made man, he, impelled by his generosity and wisdom, gave man two bags — a large one and a small one — for man to carry about with him wherever he should go or should not go. One of these bags was for man's neighbor's faults. And the other was for the man's own faults. What did man do? Which bag did he select for his neighbor's faults? Which for his own faults? And how did he carry the bags? Listen!

The man took one bag, the larger one, and fastened it securely to one end of a cord. He took the other bag, the small one, and tied it tightly to the other end of the same cord. Then, no one to compel him or to ask him to do otherwise, he flung the cord joining the bags over his shoulder in such a manner and with such dexterity that the larger bag rested on his chest and the smaller bag between his shoulders. The larger bag, the one for his neighbor's faults, was in front of the man, right before his eyes, never out of sight, never forgotten. And, holding a neighbor's faults, it was always full and overflowing.

The smaller bag, the one for the man's own faults, was behind him, right between his shoulder blades, seldom seen, usually forgotten. And this bag, this wee small bag, was always empty. All the wrong his neighbor did was always before this man. All the wrong he himself did went unnoticed and was unremembered.

There are many folks today who are, by inclination and practice and training, like this man with whom Jupiter had to do. Living in glass houses, they throw stones. Imperfect themselves, they see and bitterly condemn the imperfection of others. Themselves carnal-minded, they deplore and censure the lack of spirituality in others. Humped themselves, they ridicule the humped. Crooked themselves, they laugh at the crooked. Mockers themselves, they mock the mockers. Wrong themselves, they condemn others who are wrong. Feed them meat, they want bread. Give them bread, they want meat. Give them tea, they want coffee; give them coffee, they want ale; give them ale, they prefer wine. Offer praise, and praise is improper. Render rebuke, and rebuke is not necessary. If they do a thing that is praiseworthy, they praise themselves. It others do the same thing, it is, according to these pick-a-faults, all wrong. Picking fault with those they see on the street, picking fault with the neighbors whom they meet, picking fault at work, picking fault at play, picking fault because they cannot have their own way, picking fault with the preacher, picking fault with the pew, picking fault with as many as differ in view, picking fault with foe, picking fault with friend, until we all wish their picking fault would end. All this they do — the pick-a-faults!

They are always finding something bad in all good, something ugly in the beautiful, something false in the true.

How we need to pray: "Keep thy tongue from evil, and thy lips from speaking guile" (Ps 34:13). God keeps us from having the tongue that "speaketh proud things," that "frameth deceit," that "deviseth mischiefs like a razor," that is "bent like a bow for lies," that is as "an arrow shot out," that "boasteth great things."

In connection with the tongue we have the

TASK TRANSCENDENT

What is that task? It is the task of taming the tongue. The writer of the Epistle of James says the task is a most difficult one.

> For every kind of beasts, and of birds, and of serpents, and of things in the sea, is tamed, and hath been tamed of mankind: but the tongue can no man tame; it is an unruly evil, full of

deadly poison. Therewith bless we God, even the Father; and therewith curse we men, which are made after the similitude of God. Out of the same mouth proceedeth blessing and cursing. My brethren, these things ought not so to be (Jas. 3:7-10).

We can, with the help of God, tame the tongue so that it will speak in tenderness and not in anger, not speaking "grievous words that stir up anger," but giving the "soft answer that turneth away wrath."

The tongue can be tamed to give forth "golden gossip" that blesses rather than black gossip that wreaks havoc and brings blight. The tongue can be helpful rather than hurtful, can bring balm rather than blisters, can enrich rather than impoverish, can be pure rather than putrid, can be restraining rather than ruinous, can be faithful rather than flatterous, can be truthful rather than false, can place smiles rather than frowns on human faces, can bless God rather than blaspheme God, can be prayerful rather than promiscuous, can be as health rather than pestilence.

The tongue is the greatest power for good in the world. It electrifies the mind by its declarations of truth. It creates enthusiasm with its eloquent words of love. It rouses the whole nature by its appeal to the conscience. It is the most stirring musical instrument in the world. It is the bugle, ringing out its clarion call to duty; it is the lute, with its soft, sweet melodies of love. The tongue is the compass needle swinging truly between the two poles — and pointing out the pathway of eternal hope.

Wonderful blessing the tamed tongue can bring to many, speaking words that God approves. The tamed tongue has the power of life rather than death in it. It will bless God and not curse men. While the man with an unbridled tongue is an agent of misery and confusion, he can so tame his tongue as to be a blessing to the community, the church, the home. Such a man will know how to be silent, too, when others are hectic and frantic, having a virtuous tongue rather than a vicious tongue.

The tongue can be filled with honey, rather than being full of deadly poison. These truths are authenticated by these words:

> The tongue of the just is as choice silver: the heart of the wicked is little worth (Prov. 10:20).
>
> The tongue of the wise is health (Prov. 12:18).
>
> The Lord God hath given me the tongue of the learned, that I should know how to speak a word in season to him that is weary: he wakeneth morning by morning, he wakeneth mine ear to hear as the learned (Is. 50:4).
>
> The tongue of the wise useth knowledge aright; but the mouth of fools poureth out foolishness. . .A wholesome tongue is a tree of life: but perverseness therein is a breach in the spirit (Prov. 15: 2, 4).
>
> In her tongue is the law of kindness (Prov. 31:26).

Peter had a tongue that once spoke foolishly and cursed and denied Jesus. But that tongue was so tamed and empowered by the Holy Spirit that, at Pentecost, it was God's agent in helping to bring three thousand to their knees.

Paul had a vitrolic tongue — malicious and murderous — which spoke against Christ and commented with pleasure, no doubt, upon the death of Stephen. But, tamed by the Holy Ghost, it spoke so as to make Felix tremble.

John Knox had a tongue that was once out of God's keeping, but God so tamed it and empowered it that, in prayer, it became more alarming to a wicked queen than the bayonets of ten thousand men.

Mel Trotter once had a tongue foul and filthy, wicked and wild, which spewed out vile epithets. But this same tongue, losing half its vocabulary in conversion, became a tongue of holy fire for God.

While the untamed tongue is a world of iniquity and a deadly poison and a fagot of hell, the tamed tongue will be a tongue that prays for a soul beset by sin, that speaks peace when tempests rage, that praises God. While there is the untamed tongue that twists truths into abominable exaggerations, there is the tamed tongue that is always truthful. While there is the raucous tongue that speaks evil of others and besmirches fair names with its innuendoes of wrong and rancor, there is the tongue which, to use Milton's words, drops manna. There is the lecherous tongue with its suggestions of sensuality and its delight in foul stories, but there is also the tongue described in the words:

> Adding once more the music of the tongue
> To the sweet speech of her alluring eyes.

Though there is the untamed tongue which spreads firebrands that sets whole communities ablaze, there is the tongue, tamed of God, which is a tongue of infinite graciousness. Though there is the stammering tongue, there is also the eloquent tongue.

Hutchings tells us how the power of the eloquent tongue guided by a sincere heart has given the world immeasurable blessings. The tongue of Abraham Lincoln spoke three minutes at Gettysburg with such logical and emotional power that not a single cheer arose from the massive audience. His words, like a silver bell, will ring in the hearts of men to the end of time. The tongue of Henry Grady, stilled by untimely death when he was yet young and vigorous with ambition and hope, spoke words that brought the North and South closer together than any words that have come from human lips, before or since. So eloquent was the tongue of this young statesman that John Temple Graves said at Grady's funeral, "He sprang from a banquet hall into national fame and died, literally loving the nation back together." The tongue of Cordell Hull helped to turn the tide of suspicion in South America to trust, confidence and friendly relations toward North America. The tongue of Winston Churchill inspired patriotism, courage and fortitude in all the allied nations of the world in the darkness of the darkest days of the last world war.

What shall I more say? Nothing more say I except to beg you by the tongue of Jesus that spake words of tenderness, of righteousness, of holy and scathing denunciation, of praise, of commendation of right and condemnation of wrong, of comfort, of purity, of truth — by the use He made of His tongue, I beg you to yield your tongue to God as an instrument of righteousness.

> If any man among you seem to be religious, and bridleth not his tongue, but deceiveth his own heart, this man's religion is vain (Jas. 1:26).

Chapter Six

THE HANDS OF THE HUMAN BODY

And mine elect shall long enjoy the work of their hands
(Is. 65:22).

In speaking of the hands of the human body there are many
verses we could choose and use from the many pages of the
inspired, infallible, inerrant Word of God. But we select these
— and upon these, in the vast domain of Scriptural declarations,
we ask you to pitch your mental tents and "bide a wee":

Cleanse your hands (Jas. 4:8).

Study . . . to work with your own hands (I Thess. 4:11).

I will therefore that men pray every where, lifting up holy
hands, without wrath and doubting (I Tim. 2:8).

That they may do evil with both hands earnestly (Mic. 7:3).

Yea, ye yourselves know, that these hands have ministered
unto my necessities, and to them that were with me (Acts
20:34).

Paul, ever counting all things but loss for Christ, walking
any rough road where duty called, sailing any stormy sea as
an ambassador of God, said: "Present your members unto
God." Paul meant the members of the body.

Paul exhorted us to let our lives be a doxology unto God,
to glorify God in our bodies. *Doxasate*: the very word which is
used, or translated "glorify" is the one from which we get
our word "doxology." Thus does God teach us that we are
not only to sing the doxology in worshipful assembly but to
be a doxology wherever our bodies go, not only with our lips
but with our lives to glorify God.

93

Sad it is to learn that so many have such poor, even sordid conceptions of the glory of the human body which can be and should be a channel through which the divine becomes articulate. Some who should think deeply and speak wisely show no more wisdom when they speak of the human body than did the boy in his essay entitled "Anatomy." He wrote:

> Your head is kind of round and hard, and your branes are in it and your hair on it. Your face is the front of your head where you eat and make faces. Your neck is what keeps your head out of your collar. It's hard to keep clean.
>
> Your shoulders are sort of shelfs where you hook your suspenders on them. Your stumick is something that if you do not eat often enough it hurts, and spinach don't help it none.
>
> Your spine is a long bone in your back that keeps you from folding up. Your back is always behind you no matter how quick you turn around. Your arms you got to pitch with, and so you can reach the butter. Your fingers stick out of your hand so you can throw a curve, and add up rithmatick.
>
> Your legs is what if you have not got two of you can not get to first base, neither can your sister. Your feet are what you run on. Your toes are what always get stubbed. And that's all there is of you except what's inside, and I never saw it.

But, with no levity or leering, let us remember that the body in which the soul lives is the climax of all beauty, all completeness, all adaptation.

Our bodies were bought with a price. What price? The price paid was the precious blood of Christ, the Lamb without spots or blemish. That had to be shed in order that our bodies might become places of worship — temples of the Holy Ghost. Appropriating the finished redemptive work of Jesus to our own hearts and lives by faith, the regenerating work of the Holy Spirit takes place. He then takes up His abode in the hearts of the born-again — and their bodies become temples of the Holy Spirit.

Of this temple — this body — in which we are to glorify God, the hands, having a language as well as the mouth, are a most important part. The construction and synchronization of the human body is marvelous beyond the understanding of all scientists, because the human body, male body and female body, is the crowning glory of all God's creations.

And of all its members, so vital, so perfectly strung, the hands can be called the precision instruments. Most anyone can have an odd-looking nose, a wart, a dish face, bow legs, freckles, birthmark, pigeon toes. But there is only one kind of fingerprint to a person. No two alike. That fingerprint is precision perfect and when all other means of identification fail, the fingerprint method proves infallible. Even identical twins do not have the same fingerprints. So we see that, in the final analysis, we are really identified by our hands.

Our hands tell a story. They identify us with the kind of life we live — whether sacrificial or selfish, strong or weak, ornamental or instrumental for God. Yes, our hands commend us or condemn us. Lady Macbeth, haunted by the ghosts of her crimes and boldly placing all the guilt upon her hands, said — being horror-stricken — "All the perfumes of Arabia could not sweeten this little hand." Hands can haunt and condemn because they are the instruments of perverted thinking; and when they have served the wild schemings of the mind, they become hateful and grim reminders. Thus we see the wisdom of our yielding our hands to God as instruments of righteousness.

Let us, standing in awe in the holy and white sanctuary of the human body, consider the

WONDERS OF THE HANDS

Though we see hands often, we seldom think much upon the wonder and dignity of the hands. Do we not take the hands for granted, even though every normal human being is implemented with two of them? Do we not think of them as ordinary, prosaic, crude instruments until someone analyzes the structure and function and the marvelous mechanism of the hands? The hand has one million occupations.

Quintilian, great Roman authority on oratory, points out the limitless language of the hands in these memorable words: "Do we not ask with them, promise, call, dismiss, threaten, supplicate, detest, fear, interrogate, deny, show joy, grief, doubt, confession, repentance, and point out measure, abundance, number, and time? Amid the diversity of the languages of all peoples, the hands speak the common language of all men."

Long and technical discussions could be given of the structural character of the hands — the parts of them, the working of them, the movements of them, the skill of them, the strength and adaptability and co-ordination of action as between and among its several digits — notably the thumbs and fingers.

Virtually exhaustless is the versatility and expressiveness of the hands — mentioned about 1,440 times in the Bible. Though we are all familiar with the hand, who among us would declare that he fully understands this wondrous instrument with which man can receive or reject, beckon or repel, direct or confuse, caress or kill, soothe or stab, signal a threat or betoken a benediction? Who but God could conceive the hand's anatomy — so complete, complex, intricate, symmetrical? Who but the eternal God could make a hand "capable of the swift sweep of the keys, or that quick feeling of the pulses of a flute or the twirl of the fingers amid the strings of the harp"? Who but God, who set the members of the body where it pleased Him to set them (I Cor. 12:18), could give man the hands with which he constructs the lyre and the lute, with which he erects shrines and altars, with which he forms the various nets and snares and harnessing devices which give man dominion over the creatures of the sea, the fowls of the air, and the beasts of the field? Who but the omniscient God could conceive and construct the hands — weapons sooner loaded than any gun, sooner drawn than any sword — and make them to be "the chief executive officers of the soul," whether lifted for defense or extended for help or busied in the arts or offered in salutation or wrung in despair or spread abroad in benediction? Who but the eternal God could conceive and create the hands with which man can feel the invalid's pulse, gently wipe away the tears of a child, or cool the fevered brow, drop money into the beggar's cup, ward off missiles of injury, or, with the fingers thereof bent into a knuckled fist, become "a bolt of demolition"? Who but the eternal God could make the human arm a scepter of dominion over the world, and the hand of the arm the wonderful organ, simple in construction, the useful and indispensable instrument of the farmer, the mechanic, the artisan, the artist, the builder?

With the hands — enabling man to climb and to descend, to lift and pull down, to push and pull, to invite or drive away, to grasp or release, to weave and untie, to cleanse and besmirch, to humble and exalt, to soothe and hurt, to help and hinder, to deny and consent, to imprecate and pray, to bless and blight — man has grasped nature and subdued nature and brought out of nature all the physical conditions of civilization.

God has not given us the strength of the horse or the elephant, but He has endowed us with intelligence to apply our strength so as to surpass the power of all other creatures. God has not given us the swiftness of the eagle; some of us "fly too high" as it is. God has not given us the hearing of the elk; some of us hear too many things now. God has not given us the sight of the panther; some of us see too much already. God has not given us the keen scent of the fox hound; some of us are too busy now sticking noses in other folks' business. God has not clothed us with the dazzling plumage of the peacock; some of us now strut altogether too much in the vain shows of life. But — because of the brain having cooperation from the hand — we command forces that transport us where birds of the air cannot fly.

Formed to make and guide the plow and to construct and manage the most complicated machinery, formed so as to bring earth and rock and wood and metal into shapes and adjustments such as supply all the needs and conveniences of life, the hand subdues the earth and fashions matter into the multiform purposes of intelligent occupancy and convenience. Wielding the chisel upon shapeless marble, the hand brings forth a Venus — and "children are raised unto God from the sterile womb of stone." Manipulating a brush, the hand creates paradises upon canvass — meeting the high demands of taste and sentiment. Waving the baton, the hand "makes surging seas of tone subservient to its rod." Using tools, the hand builds ships and adjusts magnets; it spans continents criss-crossed with rivers and furrowed with valleys and bulging with mountains with iron rails over which plunge masive jugger-nauts of steel and steam. Using the instruments that the hands construct, man mounts up on steel wings that are tireless — above where soars the eagles with feathered wings that tire.

Seizing a pen, the hand writes — and the thought and wisdom and folly of the ages inhabit our libraries. When the mind desires to disseminate news and to bring the happenings of the world to our doorsteps, the hand creates type and press — and the rivulets of literature swell into rivers, flooding the world, even as the blind alleys of ignorance are changed into endless highways of wisdom. Men, smitten down with disease in the inward parts, seek to be brought back to life from the edge of the grave — and the hands of the surgeon, wielding surgical instruments, stay the onslaught of death-dealing disease.

Without the hand man's lordship over the animal kingdom would be as naught. Without this imperial instrument — the hand — man's efforts to maintain supremacy would be as futile as to expect language from a tongueless wax figure. But with the hand — and by usage of the hand — man is the throned monarch of the earth. As saith a wise man, "The hand singles man out as being designed for destinies incomparably higher than those of any species of living creature upon the earth." Yea. the hand of man sets man up and apart in exceptional and solitary dignity and distinction — placing him in such an elevation as to justify the expectations of exalted destiny in his care.

Consider the

USE OF THE WORDS "HAND" AND "HANDS" IN THE BIBLE

Everywhere in the Bible the hands are regarded as having a sacred and holy function. So in Psalm 90 the Psalmist exalts the hands as sacred, God-given instruments.

> And let the beauty of the Lord our God be upon us: and establish thou the work of our hands upon us; yea, the work of our hands establish thou it (Ps. 90:17).

We have in the Book of Acts, the story of the beginning of that beautiful service, the laying on of holy hands. It is in the New Testament, too, that we hear of wedlock, celebrated and sanctioned by the joining of hands and consecrated with the words: "What God hath joined together, let no man put asunder."

A noted journalist said: "The greatest word in the English language is 'service.' This is true; and the hands are largely the means by which service is rendered." The hands of the artist are skillful to serve mankind through the medium of beautiful pictures. The hands of the musician are delicately sensitive that they may serve mankind through the medium of inspiring music. The hands of the laborer are scarred and hard that they may serve mankind through the medium of manual labor. The hands of the doctor and surgeon are wonderfully sensitive and accurate that they may serve mankind through the medium of medical and surgical treatment. The hands of the mother are soiled and worn with the loving work of the household. Truly hands are the agents of service. What sort of hands have you — clean or dirty? — helpful or hurtful?

Pearl Boyd speaks of both kinds:

> Some hands have souls, it seems to me
> They clasp yours so comfortingly:
> You know they wish to give you cheer
> And hearten you as you draw near.
> Some hands are dead — with clammy chill —
> As if they somewhat wished you ill —
> As if they grudged the bit of touch
> Which might have meant so very much.
> Some hands present their finger tips . . .
> And even done with smiling lips,
> Can never, though well-meant, replace
> The firm hand-clasp, of old time grace.

Yield your hands — with their thirty muscles for moving the fingers of each hand, the muscles placed in the forearm and only the slender tendons running down to the fingers — as instruments of righteous service unto God.

The Bible speaks of the "hand against every man," of "the power of the hand to do hurt," of the wealth-getting hand, of the sword-wielding hand, of the bribe-receiving hand, of the hand strengthened in God, of the striking hand, of the "good hand of God," of the working hand, of the stretched-out hand, of the cunning hand, of the folded hands of those who desire sleep, of the slack hand, of the withholding hand, of the hand of evildoers, of the feeble hand, of wounded hands, of holy hands, of hands "stretched out with scorners," of hands that offend, of clean hands, of those who "do evil with both hands earnestly" (Micah 7:3).

And, thinking of these hands, and other hands mentioned in the Bible, we have

A VISION OF HANDS

Some years ago, Dr. Frank Crane wrote this of the hands: "Think of the hands of them that do the world's dirty work.

Hands of the maid who scrubs the floor, of the Slav woman mopping the hall in the office building, bleached hands of the dishwasher; strong, red hands of the washerwoman slapping, soaping, and wringing the linen; muscular hands grasping the iron, the broom-stick, the mophandle, the dust cloth, the pots and skillets. Hands upon the locomotive throttle, upon the automobile steering wheel, upon the motorcycle handle, upon the aeroplane gear — hands which if but negligent or awkward a second would bring death. Hands drawing back the bow string, pressing the trigger of the automatic revolver, manipulating the army rifle, loading the eight-inch cannon, swinging the sandbag and the lead pipe, holding the brass knuckles, the dagger, the club. Hands of crime, individual and national.

"Hands plying the whip upon little children, the cat-o-nine-tails upon the naked backs of seamen, instruments of torture upon heretics, scourging the Christ. Hands of hate.

"Hands of the surgeon creeping among the mazes of life, feeling the pulse, delivering the child, holding the hypodermic syringe, the lancet, the stethoscope.

"Hands of fair women, combing and twisting the hair, powdering the face, penciling the eyebrows, tying ribbons, patting furbelows, buttoning, hooking, marching, arranging.

"Hands plump and baby-fat; hands dry, old, veined, like a tree-trunk. Hands manicured and soft as velvet; hands gnarled, twisted, hard as leather. Hands gloved and tender; hands brown, three-fingered, scarred.

"Hands hoeing, plowing, driving, wheeling barrows. Handling pitchforks, cleaning stables, digging ditches, making gardens, cultivating farms. Hands of mothers caressing the child's cheek, of nurses smoothing hot brows, of lovers piddling palms. Hands folded in prayer, upraised in benediction, extended in excommunication. Busy hands, myriad functioned, spirit-moved, soul-impregnated, the moving semaphores of life.

Swarms of hands, fluttering as birds; beneath them spring up giant buildings, monuments, bridges, railways, the wonders of the world."

It would be terrible to be without hands — to have not those wonderful instruments to minister to the needs and comforts of the body in a cleansing and protective way — bathing the body or clothing the body or warding off hurtful attacks upon the body. But it is more terrible, viewed in the light of the judgment hour when we must "give an account of the deeds done in the body," considered in the recognition of the blessedness of the service hands can render and of the good they can perform, to have two strong and supple, uninjured, unimpaired hands — and to have yielded them to do the Devil's bidding in the Devil's work. How awful to have two functioning hands and not yield them to God as instruments of righteousness! Terrible it is to have no hands or just one hand or mangled hands or twisted hands or three-fingered hands or hands ruined by rheumatism! But more terrible it is to have two hands unwithered and unmarred, and they be hands defiled, unclean, greedy for unrighteous gain, dishonored in business dealings, performing the service of Satan, or of them who do Satan's will as those blinded by his devices and deceived by his wiles. How we need always and everywhere, to bear in our hands what Paul calls "the dying of the Lord Jesus" that it may be known of our hands on earth and recorded of our hands in heaven that they are instruments of righteousness unto God.

If we yield our hands unto God as instruments of righteousness — hands "holy and acceptable unto God" — we will so live as not to be ashamed to give answer in the closet or to shout answer from the housetop to God's question:

"WHAT IS THAT IN THINE HAND?"

God asked that question of Moses when Moses hesitated to become the Lord's messenger. Moses mentioned difficulty after difficulty which, he thought, would excuse him from entering on his allotted task. When Moses seized the serpent by the tail — in obedience to the command of God — it became a rod in his hand again. He was taught that what was formidable to weak faith might become an element of power.

Joshua, what is in thine hand? A spear. And God told him to hold it aloft — and stretch it toward Ai. Joshua, extending the spear as the signal agreed upon with the men who were in ambush, had a great victory.

In his hand, Shamgar had only an ox goad — a clumsy and rude weapon. But six hundred Philistines fell when Shamgar, with strong hand, wielded it — and Israel was delivered.

In their hands Gideon and his men had only lamps, pitchers, trumpets — strange weapons all. But against the countless Midianites God made these feeble instruments mighty for the accomplishment of His divine purpose.

In his hand Samson had only the jawbone of an ass — after "the Philistines shouted against him." But, when the Spirit of the Lord came mightily upon him, he "put forth his hand" and took that jawbone "and slew a thousand men therewith."

In his hand David once had only a harp. But with that harp he subdued for a while instincts as low as hell in the soul of King Saul. In his hand again David had only a sling and a pebble. But with that, with aim unerring and with hand made strong in the Lord, he felled Goliath and gave victory to Israel's armies.

In his hand a young lad had five loaves and two small fishes. "What are these among so many?" — so many hungry people. But with them, Jesus supplied the wants of the multitude — even as today He can take "the things which are *not*, to bring to naught the things that *are*"; even as now He can "make the foolish things of the world confound the things which are mighty."

In her hand, Mary had an alabaster box of ointment—very precious. Though Judas misinterpreted the act, though others complained critically about her deed, she, with it, the blessed Christ anointed. And Jesus, pronouncing a eulogy that forever linked her name with the name above every name, caused the fragrance of that ointment to perfume the world.

In her hand the little widow, with a body not so well-fed beneath poor raiment, dropped in two mites that day when Jesus "sat over against the treasury" and watched the people put in their gifts. And Jesus took those two mites of money, made silver and golden chariot wheels out of what was in her hand—and has taken her up and down all the highways of the world for nearly two thousand years.

In her hand Dorcas had a needle. That needle she used for the Lord's poor. But that needle, empowered of God, "wrought for her an inscription more durable than brass or marble"; and "her eulogy will be read when the victories of Roman armies and the glories of Grecian arts are forgotten."

In Martin Luther's hands were a thin parchment and a tiny hammer. "It is enough," answered Luther. Then he nailed his famous protests upon the doors of the Roman church—and the era of Reformation broke like a sunrise at midnight upon darkened Europe.

In his hand a one-time dissolute tinker, John Bunyan, languishing in jail, held a goose quill pen. But that pen, wielded by a hand that was yielded to God as an instrument of righteousness, wrote a book that crawled out from between the bars of the Bedford prison and walked, even as now it walks, more bypaths and traveled, even as now it travels, more highways, knocking at more doors and speaking to more people in their mother tongue than any book, save God's Bible.

In his hands, Carey held only some pegs and a cobbler's hammer. But, with heart aflame with love for the heathen world, and with hands yielded unto God as instruments of righteous service, he bannered the missionary idea into the churches — and world-wide missions is the result.

No matter what is in your hand — whether pen or broom or typewriter or kitchen utensil or painter's brush or carpenter's hammer or woodman's axe or manicure set or grocery basket or barber's razor or tool of iron — yield your hands to God as instruments of righteousness.

What is that in thine hand? Let it not be the dirty book — with its dirty leaves, its foul statements, its lustful insinuations, its licentious suggestions, it sewerage from some God-dishonoring presses.

What is that in thine hand? Let it not be the wine cup with its contents which mock. Let it not be the liquor bottle or glass containing that which at the last stingeth like the adder and biteth like a serpent.

What is that in thine hand? Let it not be the gamblers' tools with their "hearts" that are often the means of bruising hearts, with their "spades" which often dig down and get man's last dollar, with their "clubs" that have sometimes been the means of clubbing men into suicidal attitudes or actions, with their "diamonds" that have sometimes etched the pictures of disgrace and shame upon multitudes who never found life long enough to erase them.

How many with beautifully adorned and bejeweled hands need to pray:

> Take my hands and let them move
> At the impulse of thy love.

How we need to remember these words:

> Who shall ascend into the hill of the Lord? or who shall stand in his holy place? He that hath clean hands, and a pure heart; who hath not lifted up his soul unto vanity, nor sworn deceitfully (Ps. 24:3-4).

How we need so to see to it that our hands are instruments

of righteousness in service to God and to humanity that we can, without self-righteous boast, say:

> The Lord rewarded me according to my righteousness: according to the cleanness of my hands hath he recompensed me. For I have kept the ways of the Lord, and have not wickedly departed from my God. For all his judgments were before me, and I did not put away his statutes from me. I was also upright before him, and I kept myself from mine inquity. Therefore hath the Lord recompensed me according to my righteousness, according to the cleanness of my hands in his eyesight (Ps. 18:20-24).

What is that in thine hand? Let it not be a pen that writes slander or forgeries or lies. Let never your pen be dipped in the wicked man's mind or the Devil's sewerage. Let never an author write obscenely, skillfully veiling the evil in subtle language and suggestive phrases.

What is that in thine hand? Let it not be a typewriter that falsifies love when love is far from the heart. When I think of certain books printed and of certain pictures painted, I say that if some people do not go to hell it will be because that institution is burned out before they die. The Devil just as surely has held and does try to hold the hands of men for evil purposes as the hands of Elisha were held upon the hands of young King Joash in the long ago for righteous intent.

For his fidelity to the truth, Thomas Cranmer, Archbishop of Canterbury, was sentenced to die at the stake. But every day during his imprisonment he was offered life and liberty if only he would sign the deed of recantation. Every morning the document was spread out before him and the pen placed in his hand. Day after day he resisted the temptation. But at last Cranmer yielded.

But as soon as the horror of cruel death had been removed, he felt that he had bought the boon of life at too great a price. The death with which he had been threatened was the death of a lion. He felt it better to be a dead lion than a living dog! He held himself in contempt and abhorrence. He cowered before the faces of his fellow men. Life on such terms was intolerable. He made a recantation of his recantation. As a token of remorse, he burned to a cinder the hand with which he signed the document, the cowardly document. And then, at peace with his conscience, he embraced a fiery death with a joyful heart.

I know a man in the penitentiary for written blackmail. It would have been better for that man if he had done as Cranmer did. I know a young man today who is a victim of Ingersoll's infidelity. It would have been better for that young man if Ingersoll had taken the hand with which he wrote his hellish matter and had done with it as Cranmer did. I know a man who is serving a sentence in jail because of obscene letters he wrote. How much better it had been for him had he done with the hand that wrote the obscenity what Cranmer did. I know men who have robbed themselves of the riches of a good name through forgery — and some of them are working for Uncle Sam behind gray walls and in certain distinguishing clothes. It would have been better for them if they had done with their hands what Cranmer did.

It is so terrible to Christ that one should be besmirched by evil that He plunges into that terrific metaphor, surely the most heart-shuddering thing in Scripture, about the right hand being cut off and the right eye torn out — anything, everything — to be saved from the foul and festering pollution of sin.

> And if thy right eye offend thee, pluck it out, and cast it from thee: for it is profitable for thee that one of thy members should perish, and not that thy whole body should be cast into hell. And if thy right hand offend thee, cut if off, and cast it from thee: for it is profitable for thee that one of thy members should perish, and not that thy whole body should be cast into hell (Matt. 5:29-30).

As we think of God's goodness, we must say that hands yielded to God as instruments of righteousness will, as to God's causes that require money, be

Graciously Generous Hands

Wicked hands had Eli's sons — greedy for gain:

> And his sons walked not in his ways, but turned aside after lucre, and took bribes, and perverted judgment (I Sam. 8:3).

It is good for us to read these words:

> Behold therefore I have smitten mine hand at thy dishonest gain which thou hast made, and at thy blood which hath been in the midst of thee (Ezek. 22:13).

God speaks condemningly of hands greedy to get and miserly to give:

> For I know your manifold transgressions and your mighty sins: they afflict the just, they take a bribe, and they turn aside the poor in the gate from their right (Amos 5:12).

And God teaches that we can burglarize our own lives — can be highwaymen holding ourselves up and robbing ourselves — by having hands greedy for gain. Hearken!

> And they lay wait for their own blood; they lurk privily for their own lives. So are the ways of every one that is greedy of gain; which taketh away the life of the owners thereof (Prov. 1:18, 19).

And God promises reward to those who hate the gains of oppression and deal honestly with hands yielded to God as instruments of righteousness.

> He that walketh righteously, and speaketh uprightly; he that despiseth the gain of oppressions, that shaketh his hands from holding of bribes, that stoppeth his ears from hearing of blood, and shutteth his eyes from seeing evil; he shall dwell on high: his place of defense shall be the munitions of rocks: bread shall be given him; his waters shall be sure (Is. 33:15, 16).

When Pompeii was unearthed, a man was found with his hand clutching a bag of gold. The supposition is that he had a chance to flee and turned back and perished with his money. "Where your treasure is, there will your heart be also" (Matt. 6:21).

How many of us have hands that drop *one tenth* into God's house? Benevolence and liberality is not something that drops into our lives like a Christmas present while we sleep. It is something we develop — a grace we grow. It comes like an education, like efficiency in music, like skill in painting or speech. It grows, but what a dwarfish growth in some lives.

There are oaks in Japan two hundred years old which are still standing in flower pots. Such is the grace of giving in some lives. While others have grown to wide-branching, sheltering pavilions they are the stunted pigmies of selfishness and illiberality. The cigar man can say they spent more for cigars. The theater man can say they spent more for shows. The beauty parlor lady can say they spent more for waves. The Coca-Cola man can say they spent more for drinks. The homes of many could say that many are willing for their church to have carpets they would not think of putting on their floors.

Sam Jones said: "If God makes you, old sisters, wear in heaven what you gave to the poor on this earth, you won't go calling much the first few days." The lawyers who make out wills could say when they notice how some people never think of remembering the church in their wills, that our hands need to learn the grace of giving.

Hands yielded to God as gracious hands of generous and Scriptural giving will not withhold the tithe from God's treasury, will not hesitate in bringing that tithe to God's treasury, remembering that the liberal soul shall be made fat, remembering that we should "honor God with our substance and with the first fruits of all our increase."

And now soberly would I ask you to remember that whether you let the devil use your hands to do his works or whether you yield your hands to God as instruments of righteousness to do God's will, your hands, the hands of all of you, will be

EMPTY HANDS AT DEATH

Be not thou afraid when one is made rich, when the glory of his house is increased; for when he dieth he shall carry nothing away: his glory shall not depart after him (Ps. 49: 16-17).

And said, Naked came I out my mother's womb, and naked shall I return thither: the Lord gave and the Lord hath taken away; blessed be the name of the Lord (Job 1:21).

There is a sore evil which I have seen under the sun, namely, riches kept for the owners thereof to their hurt. But those riches perish by evil travail: and he begetteth a son, and there is nothing in his hand. As he came forth of his mother's womb, naked shall he return to go as he came, and shall take nothing of his labour, which he may carry away in his hand. And this also is a sore evil, that in all points as he came, so shall he go: and what profit hath he that hath laboured for the wind? (Eccl. 5:13-16).

But godliness with contentment is great gain. For we brought nothing into this world, and it is certain we can carry nothing out. And having food and raiment, let us be therewith content. But they that will be rich fall into temptation and a snare, and into many foolish and hurtful lusts, which drown men in destruction and perdition. For the love of money is the root of all evil: which while some coveted after, they have erred from the faith, and piercing themselves through with many sorrows. But thou, O man of God, flee these things; and follow after righteousness, godliness, faith, love, patience, meekness (I Tim. 6:6-11).

We are strangers and sojourners here as were our fathers. We are on a pilgrimage here — on a journey. And the less baggage we are hampered with the better off we are. Shrouds have no pockets. And if you do have pockets in your shroud, your arms will be too stiff for you to put your hands in them. Alexander, the Great, came to die: "Thrust my hands through my shroud that the people may see that they are empty."

I buried a man once in New Orleans who did not have a single flower on his casket, or a single mourner. I buried a man once on whose grave were flowers enough to fill an acre garden. But their hands were alike — *empty*. I have held the hands of paupers when they died. I have held the bejeweled hands of rich women when they were walking down into the waters of death. But all were alike — *empty*. Nothing but a cry we bring with us. Nothing we take with us as, with a gasp, we go. No man ever flies through the valley of the shadow in an airplane. No man ever rides through in a limousine. God help us to see our hands as they will be when folded in death — *empty*.

Now, let us find out, in the use of our hands for God,

Our Inspiration

What is that inspiration — if we be not altogether carnally minded? The inspiration is the serving and nail-scarred hands of Jesus. All through His earthly life the hands of Jesus were servants of His loving will, the representatives of His kindly thoughts, the tender ambassadors of His great heart, even as now, in His glorified body, they remain still the messengers of His grace and love. He never made His hands into a fist to strike others. He never had on His hands any finger to point in scorn at God's law. He never had the grasping hand —open to getting, closed to giving. He never had a lazy hand that wanted no work to find.

What mountains of human misery and woe would be nevermore possible if all human hands were like the hands of the Man of Nazareth. Oh, that the whole wide human race might join hands, and that His tender and holy hands might touch ours and transform them all into hands like unto His own.

Would that the cruel hands of this world, so careless and inconsiderate, were blest with His gentleness. His hands were sturdy and strong from labor in the carpenter shop, where He worked with saw and hammer and plane and chisel; but how soft and gentle were those hands to take the little children in His arms, to touch the aged and infirm with a kindliness that thrilled them with new courage and new happiness. Would that the scornful hands of this world, so ready to accuse and throw stones of hate, were as ready as His to forgive and lift and help. Sinners loved Him because He was not high-handed; He was ever reaching down a hand of hope to reach and save some struggler almost lost beneath the waves of life's stormy sea.

Those holy hands red with the scars of the crucifixion — those hands deep-wounded by the iron spikes that nailed Him to the Cross — were not clenched hands. They were open on the Cross, open on the Mount, open by the sea, open in invitation, open in warning, open in ascension, and are now gloriously open in welcome.

By His hands touching the eyes of the blind into sight, — let your hands be yielded as instruments of righteousness to Him. By His hands touching the ears of the deaf until the sound waves came rushing in, I beseech you to let your hands be yielded to Him as instruments of righteousness. By His hands touching the fevered brow into coolness, let your hands go forth as servants of sympathy. By His hands held out to sinking Peter on the water, let your hands be reached to the man and woman who is down. By His hands placed upon the loathsome leper, go thou to take the unclean, to bring them to Jesus. By His hands breaking the bread for thousands, let your hands feed the hungry. By His hands placed upon the dead, let your hands wipe away tears of sorrow. By His hands placed upon little children, let your hands lead them in the right way. By His hands that plied the scourge, let your hands be ready to serve against the Devil.

See His hands on the Cross! Place your hands in the nail-scarred hands — the hands that set the pillars of the earth in their sockets and drew the blue curtains of the night across the windows of heaven and pinned them together with star clusters. The now-pierced hands set the stars on their thrones in space and laid the first foundations of the waters. Christ's hands, holy hands, black with the bruises of the hammer, broken with nails, bloody with sacred pourings of His blood, held the weight of His body while every breath He drew was a pang of pain and every beat of His heart was a throb of agony. O, may these hands make us to say:

> Lord, when I am weary with toiling
> And burdensome seem thy commands,
> If my load should lead to complaining,
> Lord, show me thy hands,
> Thy nail-pierced hands,
> Thy cross-torn hands,
> My Saviour, show me thy hands.

Chapter Seven

THE KNEES OF HUMAN BODY

Bowing their knees (Mark 15:19).
I fell upon my knees (Ezra 9:5).
Daniel kneeled upon his knees three times a day (Dan. 6:10).
Jesus kneeled down, and prayed (Luke 22:41).

The human body has a moral use — in that it deters from doing evil things. A man's conscience might protect him if his mind impelled him to be a burglar. And a man's reason would restrain him if he had the idea to do murder. But the supreme peril of the burglar would be that he might be seen — because he would have to take his body wherever he went, and the body might be arrested and put in jail. And the great peril of the would-be-murderer is that he might be found out and his body be "hanged by the neck until dead."

The possession of bodies necessitates conventions. Bodies must be fed. Bodies must be clothed. Bodies must be sheltered. Bodies must be bathed. Basic are these demands — and to meet them men must work. In work for the demands of the body people are brought together — and their social and individual duties are inevitably blended. Farmers must cultivate farms and harvests be gathered to provide food for bodies. Sheep must be herded and sheared and cotton grown to furnish clothes for bodies. Coal must be mined and forests cut and houses built to furnish comfort for bodies. Community good and civilization's activities hinge upon the fact of bodies.

But the purpose of the body—"the beautiful, passionate

body," as Swinburne expressed it — of every "moist and un-
pleasant body," as Dickens writes — of every strong body, of
every weak body — is to glorify God. Although we are urged
to present our bodies a living sacrifice, holy and acceptable
unto God, which is our reasonable service; although we are
exhorted to refuse to let sin reign in our mortal bodies;
although we are urged to yield the members of our bodies
unto God as instruments of righteousness; although we are
told that even when we are "troubled on every side and perplexed and cast down and persecuted" we should be "always
bearing about in the body the dying of the Lord Jesus that
the life also of Jesus may be made manifest in our mortal
bodies" (II Cor. 4:6-11) — in spite of all these considerations,
we find many cheat themselves and dishonor God by refusing
and failing to "glorify God in the body," by failure to make
the body a doxology of praise unto God "in whose hand our
breath is" (Job 12:10).

Some have ears as deaf to Gospel invitation and the call
of God's commandments as the bandaged ears of an Egyptian
mummy. Some have eyes as blind to the beauty of Christ
and to open church doors and to the workings of the adver-
saries of God as have been for centuries the eyes of the Sphinx
to all the armies that marched and to all the people who have
rested in its shadow. Some have hands as useless in the
services of Christ as the armless statue of Venus is useless in
bandaging those in battle wounded. Some have lips as dumb in
giving Christian testimony as are the marble lips of a dummy.
Some have minds as unreplenished of Scriptural truth as a
dumb doll upon a ventriloquist's knee. Some have lips — in
this land of freedom of speech — which seldom form themselves to express gratitude to God for his loving kindness and
tender mercies. Some have feet that find their way to God's
sanctuaries with the frequency of snow storms in Florida.
Some, in a land where service should be rendered, put their

shoulders to no wheel and withhold their necks from honorable yokes. Some have knees that bow to Baal's altar. And some have knees that bow to God. And it is of the knees of the human body that we write.

In the Bible we read of knees that bear, of knees that bow, of knees smitten, of knees diseased, of knees bowed down, of knees slept upon, of dangling knees, of preventing knees, of unbent knees, of feeble knees, of knees in water, of knees smiting together, of mocking knees, of knees with the face between them, of Jesus' knees at which Peter worshiped. And the knees, a part of the body — the body called "the urn of the soul"—must be yielded to God as instruments of righteousness.

In the Bible to *bow* the knee signifies to worship (Rom. 11:4), to pray (Eph. 3:14), to be in subjection (Phil. 2:10).

Let us notice what the knees — as we observe the use of them in the Bible — would teach us.

In the Bible, the knees are used to show how God is glorified in

RIGHTEOUS REFUSALS

Elijah, after the great victory on Mount Carmel, went "unto Horeb the mount of God."

> And he came thither unto a cave, and lodged there; and, behold, the word of the Lord came unto him, and he said unto him, What doest thou here, Elijah? And he said, I have been very jealous for the Lord God of hosts: for the children of Israel have forsaken thy covenant, thrown down thine altars, and slain thy prophets with the sword; and I, even I only, am left; and they seek my life, to take it away (I Kings 19:9, 10).

And the Lord said unto him:

> Yet have I left me seven thousand in Israel, all the knees which have not bowed unto Baal, and every mouth which hath not kissed him (I Kings 19:18).

Though many assisted apostasy in bowing the knee to Baal, seven thousand refused to bow their knees and thus glorifed God.

In Babylon, Nebuchadnezzar the king made an image of gold, whose height was thee score cubits, and the breadth thereof six cubits, and set it up in the plane of Dura.

> Then an herald cried aloud, To you it is commanded, O people, nations, and languages, that at what time ye hear the sound of the cornet, flute, harp, sackbut, psaltery, dulcimer, and all kinds of musick, ye fall down and worship the golden image that Nebuchadnezzar the king hath set up: and whoso falleth not down and worshipeth shall the same hour be cast into the midst of a burning fiery furnace . . . certain Chaldeans came near, and accused the Jews. They spake and said to the king Nebuchadnezzar, O king, live for ever. . . . There are certain Jews whom thou hast set over the affairs of the province of Babylon, Shadrach, Meshach, and Abednego; these men, O king, have not regarded thee: they serve not thy gods, nor worship the golden image which thou hast set up" (Dan. 3:2, 4-12).

Joseph refused to bow knee to the god of lust when Potiphar's wife "cast her eyes upon Joseph."

> And it came to pass, as she spake to Joseph day by day, that he hearkened not unto her, to lie by her, or to be with her (Gen. 39:10).

Queen Vashti bowed not the knee to unrighteous display of her body.

> On the seventh day, when the heart of the king was merry with wine, he commanded Mehuman, Biztha, Harbona, Bigtha, and Abagtha, Zethar, and Carcas, the seven chamberlains that served in the presence of Ahasuerus the king, to bring Vashti the queen before the king with the crown royal, to shew the people and the princes her beauty: for she was fair to look on. But the queen Vashti refused to come at the King's commandment by his chamberlains: therefore was the king very wroth, and his anger burned in him (Esther 1:10-12).

And Moses bowed not his knees to accept Egypt's glory and evil:

> By faith Moses, when he was come to years, refused to be called the son of Pharaoh's daughter; choosing rather to suffer affliction with the people of God, than to enjoy the pleasures of sin for a season; esteeming the reproach of Christ greater

riches than the treasures in Egypt: for he had respect unto the
recompence of the reward (Heb. 11:24-26).

How we need righteous knees that will not bow to the law
of the social mob in a day when so many do like others
because "everybody does it," — because its popular to parade
in paths where God is not acknowledged.

We find in the Bible that knees teach the

FEARFULNESS OF GOD'S JUDGMENTS

This shows the prophet Nahum, "who had the tongue of a
poet, the mind of a patriot, and the heart of a Cain," in his
exultation over the impending destruction of Nineveh. Those
who have accused Nahum of being among the prophets at a
peace conference should remember that Nahum, grasping one
truth with fierce intensity, shows how God, in righteous
judgment, punishes violence, vindicates the righteous, and
punishes oppressors. Listen to his words:

> ⌈Nineveh⌉ is empty, and void, and waste: and the heart
> melteth, and the knees smite together, and much pain is in all
> loins, and the faces of them all gather blackness.
>
> Behold, I am against thee, saith the Lord of hosts, and I
> will burn her chariots in the smoke, and the sword shall devour
> thy young lions: and I will cut off thy prey from the earth,
> and the voice of thy messengers shall no more be heard (Nah.
> 2:10, 13).

In the days of Amos, when the outside of the cup was gold
and the inside was tarnished and foul, when people bowed
their knees to a strange god, the prophet showed the fearful-
ness of the judgment of God in these words:

> And he said, Amos, what seest thou? And I said, A basket
> of summer fruit. Then said the Lord unto me, The end is
> come upon my people of Israel; I will not again pass by them
> any more (Amos 8:2).

Daniel was a great man anywhere and everywhere — at
morning, noon, night, and midnight. In courage he faced the
cruel eyes and yawning jaws of lions. In courage he turned
his face from king to God in pagan Babylon. In wisdom he

rose high at Nebuchadnezzar's court. In faith he worshiped
God in his own room. In public he acknowledged God. In
idolatrous Babylon

> Belshazzar the king made a great feast to a thousand of his
> lords, and drank wine before the thousand. Belshazzar, whiles
> he tasted the wine, commanded to bring the golden and silver
> vessels which his father Nebuchadnezzar had taken out of the
> temple which was in Jerusalem; that the king, and his princes,
> his wives, and his concubines, might drink therein. Then they
> brought the golden vessels that were taken out of the temple
> of the house of God which was at Jerusalem; and the king, and
> his princes, his wives, and his concubines, drank in them. They
> drank wine, and praised the gods of gold, and of silver, of brass,
> of iron, of wood, and of stone. In the same hour came forth
> fingers of a man's hand, and wrote over against the candlestick
> upon the plaister of the wall of the king's palace: and the
> king saw the part of the hand that wrote. Then the
> king's countenance was changed, and his thoughts troubled
> him, so that the joints of his loins were loosed, and his *knees*
> smote one against another. . . . In that night was Belshazzar
> the king of the Chaldeans slain (Dan. 5:1-6, 30).

Old King Herod never bowed his knees in worship to
Christ. But listen:

> And upon a set day Herod, arrayed in royal apparel, sat upon
> his throne, and made an oration unto them. And the people
> gave a shout, saying, It is the voice of a god, and not of a man.
> And immediately the angel of the Lord smote him, because he
> gave not God the glory: and he was eaten of worms, and gave
> up the ghost (Acts 12:21-23).

In the usage of the knees, we read of knees yielded unto
Satan as instruments of unrighteousness in the

MEANNESS OF MOCKERY

"Bowing their knees (they) worshiped him" (Mark 15:19).
What mockery! The old philosopher said: "Mockery is often
the poverty of wit." Tennyson said: "He never mocks, for
mockery is the fun of little hearts."

Concerning what the people did to Jesus and said to Jesus the day of His crucifixion, what meanness of mockery we see!

> And when they had platted a crown of thorns, they put it upon his head, and a reed in his right hand: and they bowed the knee before him, and mocked him, saying, Hail, King of the Jews! (Matt. 27:29).

> And they smote him on the head with a reed, and did spit upon him, and bowing their knees worshiped him (Mark 15:19).

Let us give no obedience, — bend no knee — to gods of this world lest we be found guilty of mocking Him in worship, in attitudes, in words, in deeds. Let us not be found guilty as one who mocks the Lord, — "mocks as one whom the fen fire leads, by the creed-wrought faith of faithless souls that mock their doubts with creeds."

But another truth the knees teach us as we find it in the Bible. This is the

HUMANITY OF JESUS

Jesus kneeled and prayed (Luke 22:41). Thus we see that Jesus, though God, felt the need to pray. He knew the wisdom of getting into the private place to talk with his Father before He went to the public place to do the work God wanted Him to do.

Think of Jesus, before His incarnation on the throne, now on His knees. His birth into this world was a translation at the same time as it was an incarnation. It was a transfer of His person from a previous condition of existence to an earthly one. It was His being clothed upon with our human nature. His incarnation meant, and means, that the pre-existent Christ was embodied in human flesh, demonstrated in human life, exemplified in human action, crystalized in human form. Significant indeed the words:

> Wherefore when he cometh into the world, he saith, Sacrifice and offering thou wouldest not, but a body hast thou prepared me.

> Then said he, Lo, I come to do thy will, O God. He

taketh away the first, that he may establish the second. By the which will we are sanctified through the offering of the body of Jesus Christ once for all (Heb. 10:5, 9-10).

With the body God prepared for Him, Jesus was perfectly human, but a perfect human. As I have written in my book *Beds of Pearls* so say I again:

As man, He got tired; as God, He said "Come unto me, all ye that labour and are heavy laden, and I will give you rest" (Matt. 11:28).

As man, He got hungry; as God, He fed thousands with a lad's lunch (John 6:9).

As man, He got thirsty; as God, He gave living water (John 4:10).

As man, he prayed; as God, He made, in praying, no confession of sin.

As man, He was tempted in all points like as we are; as God, He was without sin, baffling His enemies with the question, "Which of you convinceth me of sin?" (John 8:46).

As man, He slept; as God, He arose from sleep and stilled the raging tempest.

As man, He sorrowed over separation from friends; as God, He promised never to leave them comfortless, and to come to them (John 14:18).

As man, a ship carried Him; as God, He walked on the rolling tumbling sea (John 6:19).

As man, He accepted a village girl's invitation to her wedding; as God He there changed water into wine.

As man, He was despised of men; as God, "all the angels of God worship him" (Heb. 1:6).

As man, He got lonely; as God, He said, "The Father hath not left me alone" (John 8:29).

As man, He longed for human companionship and sympathy; as God, He trod the winepress alone (Is. 63:3).

As man, He wept at Lazarus' grave; as God, He raised Lazarus from the dead.

As man, He grew in wisdom and stature; as God, He upholdeth "all things by the word of his power" (Heb. 1:3). Thinking of the humanity of Jesus as set forth by His falling upon His knees to pray, we think, as Moyer expresses it, of some wonderful contrasts concerning Christ — His human nature and His divine nature in such holy union.

He who made all things in creation was "made flesh" to provide salvation. (John 1:14).

He who made man was "made in the likeness of men" (Phil. 2:7).

He who was the Creator of the angels was made "a little lower than the angels for the suffering of death" (Heb. 2:9).

He who made the Law was "made under the Law" (Gal. 4:4).

He who was "clothed with honour and majesty" (Ps. 104:1) "was wrapped in swaddling clothes" (Luke 2:12).

He who is the Father of eternity (Is. 9:6) became an infant of days.

He who came a Babe (Luke 2:12) will come a King (Rev. 19:16).

He who upholds "all things by the word of his power" (Heb. 1:3) was upheld in the arms of Mary, and of Simeon (Luke 2:27-28).

He of whom it was stated "Behold your God!" (Is. 40:9) is the One of whom it was stated "Behold the Man!" (John 19:5).

He who "measured the waters in the hollow of his hand" (Is. 40:12) poured "water into a basin" (John 13:5).

He who was "girded with power" (Ps. 65:6) "took a towel, and girded himself" (John 13:4).

He of whom it is written, "Ten thousand times ten thousand stood before him" (Daniel 7:10), "stood before the governor" (Matt. 27:11).

He who "knew no sin" (II Cor. 5:21, who "did no sin")

(I Pet. 2:22), was "without sin" (Heb. 4:15), and in whom was "no sin" (I John 3:5) bore "our sins in his own body on the tree" (I Pet. 2:24).

But, noticing the usage of the word "knee" and the word "knees," we see, as one who sees a glorious landscape through the eye of a needle, the

Exaltation of Jesus

Jesus who was once the earth-rejected One is now the heaven-accepted One.

> And he shall send Jesus Christ, which before was preached unto you: whom the heaven must receive until the times of restitution of all things, which God hath spoken by the mouth of all his holy prophets since the world began (Acts 3:20-21).

Jesus who was once crowned with thorns is now crowned with glory and honor.

> But we see Jesus, who was made a little lower than the angels for the suffering of death, crowned with glory and honour; that he by the grace of God should taste death for every man (Heb. 2:9).

Jesus who was once on the tree — "who his own self bare our sins in his own body on the tree, that we, being dead unto sins, should live unto righteousness" (I Pet. 2:24) — is now on the throne.

> Looking unto Jesus the author and finisher of our faith; who for the joy that was set before him endured the cross, despising the shame, and is set down at the right hand of the throne of God (Heb. 12:2).

And this One now on the throne says to us:

> To him that overcometh will I grant to sit with me in my throne, even as I also overcame,, and am set down with my Father in his throne (Rev. 3:21).

Jesus who appeared to put away sin (Heb. 9:26) now appears in the presence of God for us.

> For Christ is not entered into the holy places made with hands, which are the figures of the true; but into heaven itself, now to appear in the presence of God for us (Heb. 9:24).

Jesus "once cursed on earth" is now crowned in heaven. "Jesus
. . .heaven opened. . . .on his head were many crowns" (Rev.
19:10-12). Jesus who was once the bruised One of earth is
now the blessed One in heaven. Jesus once the one under the
wrath of God — now the worshiped one of heaven.

> The four and twenty elders fall down before him that sat
> on the throne, and worship him that liveth forever and ever,
> and cast their crowns before the throne saying, Thou art
> worthy, O Lord, to receive glory and honour and power: for thou
> hast created all things, and for thy pleasure they are and were
> created (Rev. 4:10-11).

The exalted Christ!

> For it is written, As I live, saith the Lord, every knee shall
> bow to me, and every tongue shall confess to God (Rom. 14:11).
> This Jesus hath God raised up, whereof we all are witnesses.
> Therefore being by the right hand of God exalted, and having
> received of the Father the promise of the Holy Ghost, he
> hath shed forth this, which ye now see and hear (Acts 2:32-33).
> Him hath God exalted with his right hand to be a Prince
> and a Saviour, for to give repentance to Israel, and forgiveness
> of sins (Acts 5:31).
> Wherefore God also hath highly exalted him: and given
> him a name which is above every name: that at the name of
> Jesus every knee should bow, of things in heaven, and things
> in earth, and things under the earth; and that every tongue
> should confess that Jesus Christ is Lord to the glory of God
> the Father (Phil. 2:9-11).

Thinking upon Christ's glorious person, Christ's matchless
love, Christ's marvelous grace, we should say what Paul said:
"For this cause I bow my knees unto the Father of our Lord
Jesus Christ" (Eph. 3:14).

But we must not forget that the usage of the knees in the
Bible teach us the

PRACTICE OF PRAYER

> When Solomon had made an end of praying . . . he arose
> from before the altar of the Lord, from kneeling on his knees
> (I Kings 8:54).

Elijah cast himself down upon the earth, and put his face between his knees (I Kings 18:42).

And at the evening sacrifice I arose up from my heaviness; and having rent my garment and my mantle, I fell upon my knees, and spread out my hands unto the Lord my God, and said, O my God, I am ashamed and blush to lift up my face to thee, my God: for our iniquities are increased over our head, and our trespass is grown up unto the heavens (Ezra 9:5-6).

Now when Daniel knew that the writing was signed he went into his house; and his windows being open in his chamber toward Jerusalem, he kneeled upon his knees three times a day, and prayed, and gave thanks before his God, as he did aforetime (Dan. 6:10).

And they stoned Stephen, calling upon God, and saying, Lord Jesus, receive my spirit. And he kneeled down and cried with a loud voice, Lord, lay not this sin to their charge. And when he had said this, he fell asleep (Acts 7:59-60).

But Peter put them all forth, and kneeled down, and prayed; and turning him to the body said, Tabitha, arise. And she opened her eyes: and when she saw Peter, she sat up (Acts 9:40).

At Tyre, Paul found some Christians. And of what they did when Paul came unto them, while "the ship was to unlade her burden," we read:

And finding disciples, we tarried there seven days: who said to Paul through the Spirit, that he should not go to Jerusalem. And when we had accomplished those days, we departed and went our way; and they all brought us on our way, with wives and children, till we were out of the city: and we kneeled down on the shore, and prayed (Acts 21:4-5).

And of what Jesus did when he came to the garden of Gethsemane, we read:

And when he was at the place, he said unto them, Pray that ye enter not into temptation. And he was withdrawn from them about a stone's cast, and kneeled down, and prayed, saying, Father, if thou be willing, remove this cup from me: nevertheless not my will, but thine, be done (Luke 22:40-42).

And he went forward a little, and fell on the ground, and prayed that, if it were possible, the hour might pass from him (Mark 14:35).

And Jesus, in teaching as never man taught, said: "Pray ye."

We, with our mortal bodies, should see that the life of Jesus as to prayer should be made manifest in the knees of our mortal bodies by our yielding those knees as instruments of righteousness in prayer — in frequent prayer, in tireless prayer, and by praying without ceasing.

Prayerfulness is the evidence of grace, the act of dependence, the soul of expression, the harbinger of joy, the bringer of blessing, the hand of power, the killer of sin, the road to victory, the remover of rust, the breath of summer, the secret of fruitfulness, the soil of love, the developer of faith, the helper of others, and brightener of hope. Prayer brings us into touch with God, and keeps God in touch with us.

Prayer is the *delight of the saint*, the *armor of the soldier*, and the *supplier of the servant*. He who does not pray well lives ill. Many must be our bendings of knees. Many must be our trips to the prayer closet. Many must be our pleadings. Many must be our forgivings. God works when men pray. No spiritual power is existent apart from prayer. Prayer changes things within and without.

With knees kneeling in prayer beside our beds, at our tables, in our offices, in hotel rooms — in many places — let us say with Constance Calenberg:

> O Lord,
> I can not bear Thy Cross
> Beyond the city gate;
> Nor ever know, as Simon knew,
> The burden of its weight.
> I can not lean
> As John, beloved,
> With reverence on Thy breast;
> Nor walk
> As Peter walked in faith
> Across a billow's crest.
> I can not work, as Martha worked;
> Nor bring Thee ointment sweet,
> **As Mary**

Broke her costly flask
Of fragrance
At Thy feet.
I can but look to Thee in prayer,
And seek
Thy Spirit's fill —
One gift to give:
My heart and soul surrendered to Thy will!

Chapter Eight

THE FEET OF THE HUMAN BODY

*Ponder the path of thy feet . . . Remove thy foot from
evil* (Prov. 4 26, 27).
Make straight paths for your feet (Heb. 12:13).
I have refrained my feet from every evil way (Ps.
119:101).
He . . . set my feet upon a rock (Ps. 40:2).

I would have you think just now of

DOCTRINES AND DUTIES

The doctrines of Christianity relate to such subjects as the
nature and attributes of God, the relations in which God stands
to man, the relations in which man stands to God, and man's
past history, present condition, and eternal destiny. And every
true doctrine is only the assertion of a fact in regard to one
or more of these subjects.

Concerning God we have this doctrine: "God is infinite,
eternal, unchangeable in his being, wisdom, power, holiness,
justice, goodness, truth." And this doctrine is a *fact*.

Concerning man we have this doctrine: "Man fell from his
high estate in which he was created by sinning against God
and became spiritually totally depraved." And this doctrine is
a *fact*.

Concerning Jesus we have this doctrine: "There is none
other name under heaven given among men whereby we must
be saved." And this doctrine is a *fact*.

Concerning the Bible we have this doctrine: "All Scripture
is given by inspiration of God." The Bible is the inspired,

infallible, inerrant Word of God — infinite in scope, universal in interest, personal in application, regenerative in power, inexhaustive in adequacy, the miracle Book of diversity in unity. But this doctrine is also a *fact*. And that is true of all true doctrines. The doctrines of Christianity are nothing more, nothing less than the *facts* of Christianity. Thus they lie at its foundation. Doctrinal facts and factual doctrines furnish the basis for Christianity.

Now there is a relation that exists between doctrines and duties. Doctrines make for duties. Why is it my duty to love God? Certain doctrines about God being glorious in Himself and the Bestower of many blessings answer this question. If these doctrines concerning God are not facts, would there rest on our hearts the slightest obligation to fix our supreme affections on Him?

Why is it my duty to believe on the Lord Jesus Christ? Bible doctrine says that I am a lost and helpless sinner, that Jesus is the only Saviour, that Jesus commands me to believe on Him, that Jesus is worthy of all my confidence, that only by believing on Him and in Him can I be brought into that spiritual condition in which I shall be able to render to Him the worship and service of which He is infinitely worthy. And if these doctrines were not facts, would there be any reason whatever why I should give Him the supreme confidence of my soul?

The doctrines of Christianity make Christianity's duties. There is no duty imposed upon us in God's Word that is not created by one or more of the doctrines found therein. The doctrines of Christianity give rise to the Christian's duties. The duties of the Christian flow from the doctrines of Christianity.

Now in the Book of Romans, even as in all his other epistles, Paul presents doctrines and duties. In the chapters previous to the twelfth chapter, he establishes a number or doctrines — among them being the doctrine that God is infinitely merciful and has bestowed infinite mercies on the human race through

the Lord Jesus Christ. And now, in the first verse of the
twelfth chapter, he beseeches those to whom he has been
writing to perform the great duty to which those mercies give
rise:

> Present your bodies a living sacrifice, holy, acceptable unto
> God, which is your reasonable service.

These words are in harmony with the words in the sixth
chapter:

> Let not sin therefore reign in your mortal body, that ye
> should obey it in the lusts thereof . . .but yield yourselves
> unto God, as those who are alive from the dead, and your
> members as instruments of righteousness unto God.

That means, of course, that every power of the body is to
be His — the eyes His to "survey His glory in His word and
in His works"; the ears His to listen to His commands; the
mouth His to proclaim His name and celebrate His praise; the
hands His to labor for the promotion of Christ's causes; the
heart His to love God and our neighbors as ourselves; the feet
His to run in the way of His commandments; the whole body
His to serve Him in every way God shall require. That is
what Paul meant when he said: "Glorify God in your body."

I know not how to characterize the conduct of the man who
is the beneficiary of God's daily mercies and still deliberately
goes on in sin against Him. Such may be illustrated by an
historical incident. At the battle of Alma, in 1854, a wounded
Russian soldier fell into the hands of the English and was
piteously crying for water. An English captain stepped aside
from the ranks of a passing regiment and ministered to his
wants, and then hastened on to join his command. The
wounded man was much refreshed, and struggling up in the
use of the strength which that captain's kindness had brought
to him, picked up his gun, deliberately took aim, and shot him
as he passed away in the distance.

We are amazed at such base ingratitude. We are indignant.
And some would say surely such a story is fiction and not fact

—such a thing was never really done. But such is a fact in the person and life of every man who uses the strength that God every hour confers on him in service to the Devil, in indulgence of the flesh, in loving the things of the world. While God is invulnerable and no mortal wound can be inflicted on Him by any man, still there are men who use the very breath God gives them to breathe out before God words offensive to God's purity and insulting to God's majesty. The very powers of body and mind that God bequeaths, they employ in violating God's law — and the body to which God has given such powers, they move up and down on the earth right before God's face in the constant attitude of rebellion against God's authority.

But we talk today of the feet of the human body. The foot is not merely the end of the leg. It is an organ which only God could conceive and create. A man may know all about the rocks and his heart remain as hard as they. He may know all about the winds and be the sport of passions as fierce as they. He may know all about the stars and be as a meteor, whose end, after a brief and brilliant career, is to be quenched in eternal night. He may know all about the sea, and his soul resemble its troubled waters which can not rest. He may know all about the flowers and be as a hedge of thorns in the work that uplifts humanity. So also a man may know much about his body and use it as an instrument of unrighteousness in the service of the Devil! He may know all about the make-up of his feet and yet walk where he dishonors God and fails humanity in some day of real need! That I may help to prevent this I speak on "the feet" — powers that carry us as instruments of progress.

Now let us notice some

FACTS ABOUT FEET

The human foot is one of the most important parts of the body — structurally beautiful and extremely efficient — and

just as amazing in its workings as the body cells, the wonders
of respiration, the manifestations of the hands, the ductless
glands, the blood vessels, and the greatest pump in the world,
the heart. Wonderful are the movements of the feet — with
their tarsal and metatarsal bones, phalanges, the mystery of
muscle contraction, cushion system, automatic oiling system,
and powers to move up and down, with heel movement and tip
toe movement, whether in running or walking.

Doctor Dudley J. Morton, who spent over twenty-five years
studying the foot, says that, medically speaking, the foot is the
most neglected part of the human frame. No such neglect does
the foot deserve. Aside from its practical value, the foot has a
structural beauty as wonderful as any suspension bridge man
ever built. And engineers who have studied the foot go into
ecstasies about it ability to absorb shocks, endure strains,
bear weights out of all proportion to its size.

Each foot consists of twenty-six bones — so joined and
arched as to make an emtremely resilient flexible structure.
Strong ligaments hold the bones together. Tendons and
muscles control their motion. The joints, tendon channels and
little sacs called bursae contain a lubricating fluid which keeps
the working parts properly oiled.

Physiologists describe the foot by telling us of the real
section with its seven irregularly shaped bones dovetailed — the
largest one, the heel bone, resting firmly on the floor while
the other six bones rise to form an arch. Beyond are the five
metatarsals — long bones that you can feel in front of your
foot. The heads of these five metatarsals which form the ball
of the foot, rest on the ground when you walk. Extending
beyond the metatarsal heads are the shorter bones, called
phalanges, which form the framework of the toes. The heel
bones and metatarsals — not the toes — are responsible for the
tremendous job of bearing the body's weight.

So marvelously is the foot mechanism adjusted that these

small and delicate metatarsal bones can carry burdens that would stagger a piano mover. The four smaller metatarsals are no thicker than lead pencils — the largest, lying behind the big toe, being about the width of a slim cigar. When you stand, your weight is equally divided between these bones and the heels. In walking and running, however, there is an instant when one foot swings in the air, and the heel of the other foot is lifted off the ground. Then five slender bones bear your 110 pounds or your 200 pounds or your 250 pounds all by themselves.

We leave the physiological path now and come back to the Scriptures. Directly and indirectly feet are mentioned in the Bible. We read therein of feet stained with blood, feet in the mire, on the rock, in the pit, on the stairway, in the fire, in the stocks, in shoes. We read of naked feet, shod feet, wounded feet, bruised feet, broken feet, kissed feet, anointed feet, washed feet, dirty feet, impotent feet, mincing feet, destructive feet; of feet walking in ways of darkness, in the wilderness, in bypaths, in highways, in statues of the heathen, in ways of men, in vanity, in counsels of evil hearts, in the spirit, in love, in honesty, in uprightness, in the law, in the fear of God, in a straight way, in the counsel of the ungodly. We read of feet walking with wise men, with integrity, with craftiness, with slander, with scoffers, with irreverence.

Let us notice now — thinking upon the necessity of our feet to be yielded to God as instruments of righteousness — some paths to ponder. I would ask you to ponder the path of your feet as to

THE LORD'S DAY

God says:

Remember the sabbath day, to keep it holy (Ex. 8:20).

And remember that thou wast a servant in the land of Egypt, and that the Lord thy God brought thee out thence through a mighty hand and by a stretched out arm: therefore the Lord thy God commanded thee to keep the sabbath day (Deut. 5:15).

If thou turn away thy foot from the sabbath, from doing thy pleasure on my holy day; and call the sabbath a delight, the holy of the Lord, honourable; and shalt honour him, not doing thine own ways, nor finding thine own pleasure, nor speaking thine own words: then shalt thou delight thyself in the Lord; and I will cause thee to ride upon the high places of the earth, and feed thee with the heritage of Jacob thy father: for the mouth of the Lord hath spoken it (Is. 58:13-14).

The sabbath was made for man, and not man for the sabbath (Mark 2:27).

And the Sabbath which God forbade people to profane belonged to the old dispensation. As an holy institution it was transferred from the seventh day of the week to the first day of the week on the day of Christ's resurrection, and was henceforth to be known as the Lord's Day, which we are to keep holy in commemoration of Christ's finished redemptive work just as the seventh day was kept in commemoration of God's finished creation.

The seventh day was, by the wisdom of God, a Jewish institution. The first day is, by the purpose of God, a Christian institution. And as often as we observe the first day instead of the seventh as a day of rest and worship, we declare the superiority of the Christian to the Jewish dispensation; we declare that the resurrection of Christ was a greater fact in the world's history than was the creation of the earth. We, if we yield our feet to God as instruments of righteousness, to run in the way of his commandments, will not turn away our feet from the Lord's Day, from doing God's pleasure on God's holy day.

Yet, violation, desecration and disintegration of the Lord's Day are all about us. We have become lax and complacent in legislation. We have become evil in practice concerning the Lord's Day. No Lord's Day means no church. No church means no worship. No worship means the triumph of wrong.

"The sabbath was made for man" — not for one nation, one age, but for all time and for the whole race. It is not a burden imposed. It is rather a universal privilege and a universal and merciful appointment for the good of man forever. But little by little, inch by inch, bit by bit, nations and peoples and families and church members have become slack concerning the Lord's Day — until now their feet are removed from its observance, and there is widespread disregard for it abroad and careless dissipation of it, and a fearful desecration of its holiness.

The girls of Simmons College, Boston, Mass., have re-arranged the Ten Commandments in what they think is the order of importance. The Roman numerals indicate the number of each commandment as given in Exodus 20:

    V. Honor thy father and thy mother.
    VI. Thou shalt not kill.
    I. Thou shalt have no other gods before me.
    VIII. Thou shalt not steal.
    VII. Thou shalt not commit adultery.
    IX. Thou shalt not bear false witness.
    III. Thou shalt not take the name of the Lord in vain.
    II. Thou shalt not make unto thee any graven image.
    X. Thou shalt not covet.
    IV. Remember the sabbath day to keep it holy.

Think of the feet, going not on necessary errands, walking not and running not on errands of mercy, turned away from the Lord's Day — feet headed for picnic grounds and ball parks, feet trudging over golf courses, feet splashing in swimming pools, feet idle in loafing, feet going to the homes of others in disregard of the church habits of others, feet tramping unnecessarily in places of business, feet tramping around over rental property, feet running to places of amusement, feet on auto clutches, driving from one hot dog stand to another, feet not yielded to God as instruments of righteousness.

Ponder the path of your feet as to

CHURCH ATTENDANCE

David said:

> Lord, I have loved the habitation of thy house, and the place where thine honour dwelleth. . . .My foot standeth in an even place: in the congregations will I bless the Lord (Ps. 26:8, 12).

Do your feet find their way to the house of God at all? Are you one of the never-attenders? If so, you will be shamed, unless you have lost all power to blush, to read of what took place in Poland some years ago. Many men and women and young people walked fifty to two hundred miles to attend a preaching service. Many rode bicycles for three hundred miles. Still others came many miles in horse-drawn wagons.

Do you attend God's house with becoming and praiseworthy regularity? Is your testimony the testimony of the Psalmist: "I was glad when they said unto me, Let us go unto the house of the Lord"? Do you married people in a worthy way "take sweet counsel together and walk to the house of God in company"? Do you waver, when Sunday comes, between your house and God's house? Do you hesitate between the wisdom of the Word and the wisdom of the world? Do your feet stay at home or turn away while you say: "Well, I do not go to church on Sunday because I was never taught to go when I was young, so I did not form the habit"? Or do you keep your feet at home before the fire or in bed or in bedroom slippers while you say, "Well, I do not go to church on Sunday because I was made to go when I was young and it grew distasteful to me"?

Everything deteriorates in this world. The violin drops a tone. The razor loses its edge. The spark plug gathers carbon. The battery weakens. The watch runs down. We need a regular tuning, a repeated sharpening, a constant winding up. The house of God is the place in which these things are done. It is more than one less in crusade when you turn your feet

from God's house on the Lord's day. It is one more exposed
to the very dangers that preaching and Christian precept and
example are trying to obliterate.

Ponder the path of thy feet as to

WALKING IN RIGHTEOUSNESS

"Remove thy foot from evil." "Refrain thy foot from every
evil way." So make thy feet "run in the way of God's commandments" that you can say:

> Thou hast enlarged my steps under me, so that my feet did
> not slip (II Sam. 22:37).
>
> My foot hath held his steps, his way have I kept, and not
> declined (Job 23:11).
>
> For thou hast delivered my soul from death: wilt not thou
> deliver my feet from falling, that I may walk before God in
> the light of the living? (Ps. 56:13).

So walk in paths of righteousness that "thy foot shall not
stumble" (Prov. 3:23), that the Lord "shall keep thy foot
from being taken" (Prov. 3:26), that you may show wisdom
in witholding your foot from being unshod (Jer. 2:25) —
remembering that God will "guide our feet into the way of
peace" (Luke 1:79), remembering that without God's help
"he that is swift of foot shall not deliver himself (Amos 2:15),
making sure that you have "your feet shod with the preparation
of the gospel of peace" (Eph. 6:15), never forgetting "how
beautiful are the feet of them that preach the gospel of
peace, and bring glad tidings of good things" (Rom. 10:15).

Feet yielded to God as instruments of righteousness will be
found in the way of God's commandments. Feet yielded to
God as instruments of righteousness will not abide in evil
paths. Tragedies result when people turn aside from paths of
rectitude.

In II Samuel 2:18-23, we read:

> And there were three sons of Zeruiah there, Joab, and
> Abishai, and Asahel: and Asahel was as light of foot as a wild
> roe. And Asahel pursued after Abner; and in going he turned

not to the right hand nor to the left from following Abner.
Then Abner looked behind him, and said, Art thou Asahel?
And he answered, I am. And Abner said to him, Turn thee
aside to thy right hand or to thy left, and lay thee hold on
one of the young men, and take thee his armour. But Asahel
would not turn aside from following of him. And Abner
said again to Asahel, Turn thee aside from following me:
wherefore should I smite thee to the ground? how then should I
hold up my face to Joab thy brother? Howbeit he refused to
turn aside; wherefore Abner with the hinder end of the spear
smote him under the fifth rib, that the spear came out behind
him; and he fell down there, and died in the same place: and
it came to pass, that as many as came to the place where
Asahel fell down and died stood still.

But greater tragedies than this recorded in Holy Writ are read
of in our newspapers every day, because people walk in
paths and run in courses that displease God.

How sad for a strong man to lose a foot, or two feet. How
sad for a graceful woman to have both feet mangled, or just
one part of a foot crushed. How sad to see people once
strong now hobbling on crutches or pushed in wheel chairs.
How sad to see a man feel for a lifetime the handicap of a
club foot. But sadder far and far more tragic it is to see people
with two good, well-shod feet running with the Devil's crowd,
running with the God-hating, church-forsaking crowd, all the
while blind to the fact that they are running from the sunrise
toward the midnight, from liberty to jail, from the throne of
God to Satan's gallows, from calm to storm, from riches to
rags, from life to death.

Atalanta was a great athlete. She felt herself to be the
swiftest runner in the land. She had many suitors, for she
was very beautiful. But having been warned that marriage
would be her ruin, she saw her way of escape in offering her
hand to that suitor who would beat her in a footrace. Said
she, "I will be the prize of him who will conquer me in a
race; but death must be the penalty of all who try and fail."

Scores of young men entered the contest in spite of the hard condition. One after another they were defeated, and they were put to death without mercy. Hippomenes, a splendid and most handsome youth, thought it very rash that anyone should risk so much for a wife, but when he saw Atalanta he changed his mind and offered himself for the contest, although it did not look as though he had any chance of winning.

The race started, and the contestants flew around the course. Atalanta easily out-distanced her competitor, although she almost wished he might defeat her, for he was so young and handsome. Now Hippomenes had calculated more wisely than Atalanta knew. He had taken with him into the race, three golden apples, which he carried in concealment. He spun one of the apples along the course in front of the maiden. Atalanta was all amazement; she wanted the glittering thing. Thinking she had an easy victory, she stopped to pick it up, and Hippomenes shot ahead of her. The spectators cheered him on, but Atalanta was soon in advance once more. He threw a second apple, this time off a little to one side, and a second time the maiden determined to secure the apple, and left the course to do it. Again her suitor ran ahead, but again Atalanta came up and passed. But now the goal was near. Atalnata was weighted with the two apples, and Hippomenes was correspondingly lighter. He threw the last golden apple. She looked at it and hesitated, but again did the lust of greed take possession of her, and she stopped to gather up the third golden ball. Hippomenes, lightened by the absence of the weight, taking advantage of Atalanta's delay, flew away in advance to the goal that was just before. He won the race; he won a bride; and the story says her kingdom went with her.

But it was a union Atalanta despised. She would rather have embraced death than a husband. Many a maiden and many a youth has entered the course of life full of beauty and powers, but has trifled with sin, has let his or her feet follow the world-thrown apples of enticement and evil indulgences.

What say I now? I say the world, the flesh, the Devil will try to entice you to run in evil ways. The golden apples will glitter before you. There is but one thing to do. Ponder the path of thy feet. Keep your eye on the goal. — Looking unto Jesus the Author and Finisher of our faith, "so run that ye may obtain."

Ponder the path of the feet as to the

ALLUREMENTS OF UNCHRISTIAN WOMEN

Notice this which was written about Solomon:

> Among many nations was there no king like him, who was beloved of his God, and God made him king over all Israel: Nevertheless even him did outlandish women cause to sin (Neh. 13:26).

And Solomon, speaking from the depths of bitter experience says:

> Say unto wisdom, Thou art my sister; and call understanding thy kinswoman: that they may keep thee from the strange woman, from the stranger which flattereth with her words (Prov. 7:4-5)

Solomon knew what he was talking about when, grown old, "his wives turning away his heart after other gods," he said: "Give not thy strength unto women" (Prov. 31:3). No foolish words to be laughed at said he when he warned "The adultress will hunt for the precious life." Wisely spake he, as one burned by fire taken into his bosom, when he said of the man whose feet follow after the evil woman: "But he knoweth not that the dead are there; and that her guests are in the depths of hell" (Prov. 9:18).

Though we may wince under some of the plain language Solomon uses, we should be wise as to his words when he pictures a young man turning his feet in the path of the strange woman who ever is "a deep ditch" and " a narrow pit," "who increaseth transgressors among men" (Prov. 23:27-29).

Listen to Proverbs 7:21-27:

> With her much fair speech she caused him to yield, with the flattering of her lips she forced him. He goeth after her straightway, as an ox goeth to the slaughter, or as a fool to the correction of the stocks; till a dart strike through his liver; as a bird hasteth to the snare, and knoweth not that it is for his life. Hearken unto me now therefore, O ye children, and attend to the words of my mouth. Let not thine heart decline to her ways, go not astray in her paths. For she hath cast down many wounded: yea, many strong men have been slain by her. Her house is the way to hell, going down to the chambers of death.

To which we would add the poet's insistently sober words:

> A woman is waiting for you, my lad —
> > Ride past!
> Her cheeks are soft and her mouth is glad —
> > Ride past!
> For the flash of her glance is the light of bane,
> And the touch of her lips is the key to pain,
> And she calls to the wise man — all in vain!
> But youth is strong and will find no wrong
> In the lilting lure of her ancient song.
> And the thing that's art, and thing that's heart,
> Only the knowing can tell apart;
> And the price of the knowledge is black with stain,
> And the seed of the wisdom, bad.
>
> She would barter her love for your own, my lad —
> > Ride past!
> But your love is good and her love is bad —
> > Ride past!
> She offers the fruit of the bitter tree,
> Her kiss is the promise of misery,
> Of death and of woe; let her be! let her be!
> Youth is bold and of eager mold,
> And brass in the ken of youth is gold,
> And the acid of grief is the only test
> For the tawdry tinsel within her breast —
> Which only the eyes of the wise can see —
> And the eyes of the wise are sad!

And now, let us without levity and undue severity, ponder the path of our feet as to

THE DANCE

I do not want to condemn anyone, but to convince. I speak not to destroy but to save, not to shun one of the issues of the day but to face facts as they are, not to intrude on anyone's "rights," but to see the righteousness of God. But lovingly, yet with frankness, I say that if our feet are yielded to God as instruments of righteousness, they will not be dancing feet. No matter what objection such words meet with, no matter by what arguments assaulted, I say the dance is not Christian. You cannot make it Christian by chaperones or environment. You cannot make it spiritual by holding it in a church. You cannot hitch a dancing body and spiritual life together anymore than you can hitch a wolf and a lamb or a serpent and a lion to the same carriage. I want to see you young people attain the highest heights, have and hold the best treasure, possess spiritual power, have sweetest joys. This you can never have if your feet become entangled in the dance net or go to places where filth is felt. Spiritual power and dancing do not go together, no matter how decently the dance may be conducted. The modern dance of today is an enemy of the home, an enemy of the church, and an enemy of civilization and spirituality.

Attorney General Clifford G. Ross of Chicago has said: "Perhaps more girls have traveled to their ruin over the smooth glistening floor of the innocent-looking dance halls than any other!"

Feet yielded to God as instruments of righteousness are careful to walk in the ways of righteousness. Feet that bear the marks of the Lord Jesus are careful where they walk. It is not without significance that only parts of the body Jesus washed were the feet of his disciples; and feet that have been washed by Jesus can never move amid the slime of the world.

Someone asks: "Preacher, don't you know some ladies that dance?" Yes — some sweet, lovely little ladies, but not one of them I know has power as a soul-winner! "Do you not know some gentlemen who dance?" Yes, but I do not know one with heaven-sent blessed spiritual power. There may be some; but I say I do not know them! And I have the privilege of saying, as a physician who gives bitter medicine, that I do not believe that spiritual power in the home and spiritual power in the church and the dance travel together! Much dance in the heels is evidence of little real spiritual power in the life! "The greatest shield to virtue is modesty, the greatest destroyer of modesty is sex familiarity, and in no society outside of a brothel is such familiarity tolerated as in the dance."

To say that spirituality goes along with so-called high-class dances is like saying a pig pen is a good place for lilies. To say that there are high class dances is like saying there is high class liquor drinking. The Devil gets his work done through serge and silk as well as through calico and overalls. He tries every means to deceive you, and one of his favorite ways is to blindfold parents to believe their sons and daughters are above reproach and just a bit better than the unfortunates who have fallen morally and spiritually.

There are dances and *dances,* we admit. That some dances are not as vile and vicious as others in an axiomatic fact. But there is poison and poison — and I do not want to make a mistake and take any of it. There are snakes and snakes, but I have no use for any kind of snakes. There may be and are, I doubt not, those who may dance without dancing being their downfall. But your example may lead others into the dance whose will power is not so great, whose innocence is more easily imperiled, and whose endowment of stamina of character is not so marked.

Forget not that it is the function of the strong to protect the weak. Will an active Christian have time to dance? Will not a sensible Christian find something better to do than to dance? Will not a loving Christian feel that he cannot dance? Will a spiritually minded and soul-winning Christian have any desire to dance? "Ponder the path of thy feet."

But I would ask you now to ponder the path of thy feet as to

God's Knowledge of Man's Whereabouts

Stand in awe as David speaks of this knowledge:

> O Lord, thou hast searched me, and known me. Thou knowest my downsitting and mine uprising, thou understandest my thought afar off. Thou compassest my path and my lying down, and art acquainted with all my ways. For there is not a word in my tongue, but, lo, O Lord, thou knowest it altogether (Ps. 139:1-4).
>
> If I say, Surely the darkness shall cover me; even the night shall be light about me. Yea, the darkness hideth not from thee; but the night shineth as the day: the darkness and the light are both alike to thee. For thou hast possessed my reins: thou hast covered me in my mother's womb (Ps. 139:11-13).

The Bible says much about where a man should walk and how he should walk. Job asks this question: "Doth not he see my ways, and count all my steps?" (Job 31:4).

If our feet, yielded to Satan as instruments of unrighteousness, go to the saloon, God counts their steps. Be it to the dance hall — He counts. Be it to the house of evil — He counts. Be it to the gambler's den — He counts. Be it to visit the sick — He counts. Be it to the battlefield — He counts. Be it to a funeral — He counts. Be it to a wedding — He counts. Be it to church — He counts. If we walk staggeringly in drunkenness, God counts. If we walk strugglingly as an athlete in strenuous combat, God counts. If we walk swiftly as in the swirls of the waltz, God counts. If we walk cowardly away from duty, God counts. If we walk stealthily to haunts where virtue is an outlaw and debauchery holds orgies, God counts. If we walk to visit the sick, God counts. And all our footsteps will testify in our behalf or testify against us in that day when we stand before God to give an account of the deeds done in the body.

I beg you that you yield your feet to God as instruments of righteousness so that you will not be ashamed of the record made on earth and known in heaven. As to your feet, as to the enticements of evil paths, let them be, as said Sir Francis Burnand of his friend: "His feet were like icicles in refrigerator stockings."

Look you, with your two good feet, at the man on crutches or in the wheel chair or limping through life — and ask God if you are grateful that you do not have to go halt through life. You who go to wrong places, would you do so if you were crippled? If you were crippled, would you promise God you would go to the movie on Sunday night or to the evil place if only He would give you feet and enable you to walk? Would you? Would you dare to pray like that? Look at that club foot and ask yourself if you would promise God you would run away from church if he would heal it, were it your foot.

Now ponder the path of thy feet as to

THE BIBLE

The Psalmist said: "Thy Word is a lamp unto my feet, and a light unto my path" (Ps. 119:105).

We need to remember what a dying infidel said as he laid his trembling and emaciated hand on the Bible: "The only objection against this book is a bad life."

The Bible, a true record of God's dealings with men, is an infallible guide. The Bible, inbreathed of God, furnishes for childhood the most satisfactory spiritual truth, understandable to the child mind. The stories of the Bible and the Gospel furnish the most developing lines of teaching possible to child life. Character formation, experienced earlier than many people believe, is assisted, if not assured, for the young by Bible reading and study.

For older people, nothing can possibly furnish the incentive to honorable conduct, to high thinking, to holy living that manifests the life of Jesus in the mortal body that the Bible does. No matter what a man's condition may be, no matter what the occupation may be, the Bible speaks with a directness that leaves no uncertainty as to the duty and no doubt as to destiny.

The Bible meets the crises of life with unquestioned success. The Bible, never to be outgrown, is never out-of-date. The most up-to-date book in any library, the Bible is forever inexhaustive in adequacy. Meaningless — comparatively — would be the world's libraries without its teaching. There are no problems it cannot solve, no burdens it does not lighten, no trouble it does not lessen, no doubt assailing Christian faith it does not vanquish. There is no weariness the Bible does not help remove, no grief it cannot console, no sin it does not condemn, no righteous deed it does not commend, no defilement it cannot cleanse. The softest pillow for the dying, the mightiest spur to the living, it furnishes to the weak power, to the strong greater strength, to the hopeless renewed assurance. Not one of its promises can ever fail, not one of its fires ever die out. The guarantees it gives of eternal life are unequivocal and entirely reliable.

Let us be able to say what the Psalmist said: "I turned my feet unto thy testimonies" (Ps. 119:59).

Finally, let all men ponder the path of their feet as to

The Example of Jesus

The feet of Jesus were serving feet. Jesus "went about doing good." He walked where David rode, where Solomon rode, where Ahab rode, where Jehu rode, where kings of earth rode. But, walking the dusty highway, he traveled the best — journeyed as journeys God. Ask the blind if that be not true. Ask the beggars. Ask the deaf. Ask the sick. Ask others in distress. They will tell you that he who *walked* in doing good to others, journeyed more gloriously than kings who *rode* for selfish pleasure in pomp and power.

Faithful feet His in visiting the sanctuary. "He went as was his custom into the synagogue on the sabbath day." He loved to walk the meadows where the green grass blades were emerald strings on which the south winds played resurrection melodies. He loved to walk the roads through little towns. He loved to walk by the white shores of blue Galilee. He loved to walk the desert paths that led away from the haunts of men. He loved to walk among the woods where He could get alone with God. He loved to walk the bulging billows of the stormy lake. But He loved much more to walk the paths that led to the village synagogues and the roads that led to the temple in Jerusalem. As to attending the sanctuary of God, many feet among us need to be yielded to God as instruments of righteousness.

Frequently the feet of Jesus found the ways that led to those in trouble. To the house of Jairus they went, for great grief was there. To the home at Bethany they went, for the shadows of death were there. To the little town of Nain they went, for bereavement because of death was there. To the sea where the winds and waves buffeted His disciples they went. To the well of Sychar where a woman — dirty toy of dirty men — was, they went. His feet were feet of visitation. Our feet need to be that kind, going with a readiness which is born of gospel urgency as heat is born of the sun, going with a readiness to take the highways and the bypaths, broad streets and narrow streets, tenement stairways and muddy road, to carry the message of hope and love, being swift and jubilant to go anywhere to those in spiritual bondage, in shadows of trouble, in the gloom of despondency, in the maimings of sin, in the brokenness of defeat, in the pathos of self-disparagement, in the furnace of pain.

There are those who need their lamps replenished with the oil of joy and relit with the flame of hope. Those there are who need their hearthstones renewed with fires of blessed warmth and confidence. Those there are who need to hear a new dawning and of radiant tomorrows. How beautiful upon the mountains, in the valleys, in the slums, in the kitchens, in the fields, n the cities, are the feet of them that bring oil to empty lamps, fuel to dying fires, and cheer to the cold haunts of despair. The feet of Jesus went to the Cross — and there with the cruel nails were torn. On Calvary I hear the mockers mocking. I hear the sound of hammers. I hear the drip of blood.

> See from His hands, His head, His feet,
> Sorrow and love flow mingled down;
> Did e'er such love and sorrow meet,
> Or thorns compose so rich a crown?
> Never!

And now let me put this urge upon your heart. By His feet that went to the house of mourning, by His feet that shunned not to stop for the poor and lame, by His feet that walked to the house where slept the dead, by His feet blistered by the mountain way, by His feet that paused while he gave sight to the blind, by His feet wearied by Judea's roads, by His feet dust-covered in roads where the king's chariot whirled, by His feet laved in Galilee's waters, by His feet kissed by a woman and wiped with the hair of her head, by His feet that found their way to the garden of prayer, by His feet that walked amid His enemies in the courts of the Temple, by His feet at which the disciples in worship kneeled, by His feet that walked the last foot of the rough steeps of Calvary, by His feet punctured with nails and fastened to the Cross, I beg you to make your feet instruments of righteousness in His service.

Pray to God, saying:

> Take my feet and let them be
> Swift and beautiful for Thee

God has promised to be with us and keep us in all places, to walk with us to the last foot of the last mile of Life's journey. Treasure these words: "The Lord God is a sun and shield. . . no good thing will he withhold from them that walk uprightly." "Though I walk through the valley of the shadow of death, I will fear no evil." "Teach me, O God, I will walk in thy truth." "He is a buckler to them that walk uprightly." "They that wait upon the Lord shall. . .walk and not faint." "He that followeth me shall not walk in darkness, but shall have the light of life." "He that walketh uprightly walketh surely."

And looking beyond this world with its sickness to the world where sickness is never known, beyond this world with its darkness to the world where there is no night, beyond this world with its sin and shame to the world where nothing that defileth ever entereth, beyond this world with its death to the world where no death enters, let us yield our feet unto Him as instruments of righteousness so that when we shall see Jesus we shall know all He means when He says: "They shall walk with me in white."

Chapter Nine

THE HEART OF THE HUMAN BODY

Create in me a clean heart, O God (Ps. 51:10).

Keep thy heart with all diligence; for out of it are the issues of life (Prov. 4:23).

For from within, out of the heart of men, proceed evil thoughts, adulteries, fornications, murders, thefts, covetousness, wickedness, deceit, lasciviousness, an evil eye, blasphemy, pride, foolishness: all these evil things come from within, and defile the man (Mark 7:21-23).

But the Lord said unto Samuel, Look not on his countenance, or on the height of his stature; because I have refused him: for the Lord seeth not as man seeth; for man looketh on the outward appearance, but the Lord looketh on the heart (I Sam. 16:7).

O generation of vipers, how can ye, being evil, speak good things? for out of the abundance of the heart the mouth speaketh (Matt. 12:34).

DEFINITION OF THE HEART

What would the physiologist say the heart is? This, I suppose: "The heart is the central organ of the vascular system, a hollow muscular structure that propels the blood by alternate contractions and dilations."

Common usage would set forth the heart as the seat of the affections and passions as distinguished from the intellect and will, or the emotional nature.

Literary usage would declare that the human heart is the source of wit, courage, grief, pleasure — and kindred emotions.

The heart is used in the Scripture as the figure of the seat of man's moral being — the center and the source of the outward life, the character and the motives and the love from which the actions flow as from a fountain. Its natural character is said to be deceitful and desperately, or incurably, wicked (Jer. 17:9).

Our Lord teaches that the heart is the fountain from which flow the issues of life (Matt. 15:19). That means the thought, conduct and speech of man come from the heart. And it is a veritable cesspool of evil unless controlled by the Holy Spirit.

Let us note the

PHYSIOLOGICAL HEART

By this I mean what the physiologist tells us of the physical heart. And here we have revealed to us wonders beyond words fully to portray. The heart, a mass of muscle, weighing only about three-quarters of a pound, has the hardest job of any organ in the body. Hold out your hand, clench the fingers into a fist. Let the fingers relax slightly, then squeeze them together powerfully. Imagine yourself repeating this operation seventy times a minute, unremittingly, hour after hour, from long before your birth to the instant of your death. That is the appalling assignment of the human heart, a task which it performs so uncomplainingly that few of us are aware of its burden until we run upstairs too fast or until our physician wags his stethosope at a mitral murmur. The heart beats or contracts from 60 to 80 times a minute — or an average of 72 times a minute, 4,320 times an hour, some 100,000 times a day, or 40,000,000 times a year. Dr. Arthur I. Brown says it exerts enough energy every twenty four hours to raise a two-pound weight twelve miles in the air.

The task of the heart is to keep blood moving through the body. Like the pumping station which keeps water flowing through the mains of a city, the heart forces blood through the body's arteries and veins. The arteries carry oxygen-charged blood pumped fresh from the lungs; the veins return turgid, venous blood for purification. Connecting the arteries and veins is a spongy mass of minute vessels, the capillaries, interlacing among the cells. They are inconceivably numerous. No part of the body can be cut without puncturing one or more of them. Opened and spread out, they would cover a plot of ground 240 feet square — about three thousand times the surface of the body. End to end, the capillaries would extend four times around the earth — would fall only a few thousand miles short of reaching half the distance to the moon. Through this amazingly complex and elastic system of pipelines the heart pumps blood continuously more than ten tons every twenty-four hours.

Normally, the heart forces about five quarts of the body's blood through the circulatory system about once a minute. This can fluctuate from four quarts a minute when the body is at rest, and nine quarts a minute when in moderate exercise, up to sixteen quarts a minute during violent exercise or exertion. A drop of blood can make its round trip through the circulatory system in twenty-two seconds.

The heart, performing each day work equivalent to lifting a one-ton elevator to a height of eight stories, keeps going this river of blood in the body. On that stream are five million little boats, corpuscles and what-not that are constantly at work — loading and unloading, fighting, uniting, dividing, carrying on commerce, building and wrecking, bringing up brick and mortar as it were, for the various works along the banks and taking away debris. Day in and day out this faithful handmaiden of the body works, while we work, while we play, when we eat, when we rest, when we run, when we are mean, when we are good. How we abuse it! How we over-work it! How we make it hard for it to do its work!

But I would have us think now of what we may appropriately call the

SCRIPTURAL HEART
The Scripture speaks of many kinds of hearts — such as faint

heart, foolish heart, willing heart, proud heart, wise heart, pure heart, discouraged heart, set heart, astonished heart, hard heart, glad heart, stout heart, trembling heart, fearful heart, failing heart, rebellious heart, merry heart, contrite heart, hating heart, rash heart, understanding heart, whorish heart, large heart, stony heart, perfect heart, new heart, double heart, lowly heart, sad heart, meek heart, hypocritical heart, slow heart, broken heart, congealed heart. froward heart, whole heart, subtle heart, clean heart, perverse heart, deceitful heart, heavy heart, sound heart, enlarged heart — and other kinds which I shall not now mention.

But — what is the Scriptural heart? What does the Bible mean when it speaks of the heart? It means more than that little fleshly engine of energy within the breast, which pumps blood through the arterial system of the body. What does the Bible mean when it says: "Keep thy heart with all diligence, for out of it are the issues of life"? What does God mean when he says: "Give me thy heart"? What did David mean when he said: "Create in me a clean heart"? When Paul said to Simon Magus, "Thy heart is not right with God", did he mean Simon's heart was a physically diseased heart? No.

The heart consists of the intellect, the sensibilities, the will and the conscience — not just the engine of energy within the breast, rather one's entire emotional nature and understanding.

The heart *thinks*:

> For the word of God is quick, and powerful, and sharper than any twoedged sword, piercing even to the diving asunder of soul and spirit, and of the joints and morrow, and is a discerner of the thoughts and intents of the heart (Heb. 4:12).
> And Jesus knowing their thoughts said, Wherefore think ye evil in your heart? (Matt. 9:4).

The heart *reasons*:

> But there were certain of the scribes sitting there, and reasoning in their hearts, Why doth this man thus speak blasphemies? who can forgive sins but God only? And immedi-

ately when Jesus perceived in his spirit that they so reasoned within themselves, he said unto them, Why reason ye these things in your hearts? (Mark 2:6-8).

The heart *understands*:

For this people's heart is waxed gross, and their ears are dull of hearing, and their eyes they have closed; lest at any time they should see with their eyes, and hear with their ears, and should understand with their heart, and should be converted and I should heal them (Matt. 13:15).

The heart *believes*:

That if thou shalt confess with thy mouth the Lord Jesus, and shalt believe in thine heart that God hath raised him from the dead, thou shalt be saved. For with the heart man believeth unto righteousness; and with the mouth confession is made unto salvation. For the Scripture saith, Whosoever believeth on him shall not be ashamed (Rom. 10:9-11).

Since the intellect thinks, reasons, understands, believes, we know that it is included in the heart. As to thinking, reasoning, understanding, believing, how many intellects are wrong! The heart has *sensibilities*. These sensibilities express love and anguish, and denote feeling.

Master, which is the great commandment in the law? Jesus said unto him, Thou shalt love the Lord thy God with all thy heart, and with all thy soul, and with all thy mind. This is the first and great commandment. And the second is like unto it, Thou shalt love thy neighbour as thyself (Matt. 22:36-39).

For out of much affliction and anguish of heart I wrote unto you with many tears; not that ye should be grieved, but that ye might know the love which I have more abundantly unto you (II Cor. 2:4).

These Scriptures show conclusively that with the heart we love, and that the heart has anguish.

The heart *wills, purposes, determines*:

Who, when he came, and had seen the grace of God, was glad, and exhorted them all, that with purpose of heart they would cleave unto the Lord. (Acts 11:23).

Every man according as he purposeth in his heart, so let him give; not grudgingly, or of necessity: for God loveth a cheerful giver (II Cor. 9:7).

These Scriptures show that the heart wills and purposes.

The heart is the *seat of conscience*:

> Now when they heard this, they were pricked in their heart, and said unto Peter and to the rest of the apostles, Men and brethren, what shall we do? (Acts 2:37)

> For if our heart condemn us, God is greater than our heart, and knoweth all things. Beloved, if our heart condemn us not, then have we confidence toward God (I John 3:20-21).

Again, when Peter was preaching in Jerusalem, he discussed the exaltation of Christ: "When they heard that, they were cut to the heart, and took counsel to slay them" (Acts 5:33). Here we see the conscience can be pricked, condemned, cut. So when God says, "Keep thy heart with all diligence," God is asking that we keep our intellects, our sensibilities, our wills, our conscience, according to His will and righteousness. When he says, "Give me thine heart," God is asking that we give to Him our intellects to think as He would have us, to reason as He would have us to reason, to understand as He would have us. He asks for our sensibilities, so that we may love according to His standard. He asks for our wills so that we may do His will.

I think Dr. Crane must have had this Scriptural conception of the heart when he wrote: "The human heart is a wide moor under a dull sky, with voices of invisible birds calling in the distance. The human heart is a lonely lane in the evening, and two lovers are walking down it, whispering and lingering. The human heart is a great green tree, and many strange birds come and sing in its branches; a few build nests, but most are from far lands north and south, and never come again. The human heart is a deep still pool; in its depths are fishes of gold and silver, dancing playfully, and slow-heaving slimy monsters, and tarnished treasure hoards, the infinite animalcular life; but when you look down at it you see but your own reflected face.

The human heart is an undiscovered country; men and women are forever perishing as they explore its wilds. The human heart is an egg; and out of it are hatched this world and heaven and hell. The human heart is a tangled wood wherein no man knows his way. The human heart is a roaring forge where night and day the smiths are busy fashioning swords and silver cups, mitres and engine-wheels, the tools of labor, and the gauds of precedence. The human heart is a garden, wherein grow weeds of memory and blooms of hope, and the snow falls at last and covers all. The human heart is a meadow full of fireflies, a summer western sky of shimmering distant lightnings, a shore set round with flashing lighthouses, far-away voices calling what we can not understand. The human heart is a band playing in a park at a distance; we see the crowds listening, but we catch but fragments of the music now and again, and can not make out the tune. The human heart is a great city, teeming with myriad people, full of business and mighty doings, and we wander its crowded streets unutterably alone; we do not know what it is all about. The human heart to youth is a fairy-land of adventure, to old age it is a sitting-room where one knows his way in the dark. The human heart is a cup of love, where some find life and zest, and some drunkenness and death. The human heart is the throne of God, the council-chamber of the devil, the dwelling of angels, the vile hearth of witches' Sabbaths, the nursery of sweet children, the blood-spattered scene of nameless tragedies.

"Listen! You will hear mothers' lullabies, mad men's shrieks, hymns of Christ, the roaring of lynch mobs, the kisses of lovers, the curses of pirates. Bend close! You will smell the lily fragrance of love, the stench of lust; now odors as exquisite as the very spirit of violets, and now such nauseous repulsions as words cannot tell. Nobilities, indecencies, heroic impulses, cowardly ravings, good and bad, white and black — the mystery of mysteries, the central island nescience in a sea of science, the dark spot in the lighted room of knowledge, the unknown quantity, the X in the universal problem."

And now let us consider the importance of the

KEPT HEART

We are urged to keep the heart will all diligence. Why? Because "out of the heart are the issues of life." Jesus said:

> For from within, out of the heart of men, proceed evil thoughts, adulteries, fornications, murders, thefts, covetousness, wickedness, deceit, lasciviousness, an evil eye, blasphemy, pride, foolishness: all these evil things come from within, and defile the man (Mark 7:21-23).

> For out of *the heart* proceed evil thoughts, murders, adulteries, fornications, thefts, false witness, blasphemies (Matt 15:19).

When a man's heart is vile, his hands will be unclean. When a man's heart is crooked, his feet will walk in crooked ways. When a man's heart is wrong, he will have ears dull and deaf and fat to the voice of God. When a man's heart lacks spiritual vision, his eyes will be evil eyes. Before the hand of the thief stole, the thievery was in the heart. Before a man went his way after an evil woman, the lust was in his heart. Before the tongue moved to profanity or blasphemy, profanity and blasphemy were in the heart. Before the ear gave heed to a naughty tongue that malignity was in the heart. Before the eye got out of its calling and out of God's keeping, that which caused it so to be was in the heart. Before the knee refused to bow in prayer, that irreverence was in the heart. Before the shoulder refused to receive a load and carry it for God, that refusal was in the heart. Before the neck was withheld from the yoke of God, the stubbornness was in the heart. The *heart* is the birthplace of all the evils that other members of the body do. The *heart* is the incubator in which the Devil hatches out his foul plots.

The supremacy of the heart kept for Christ must ever be recognized since the heart is center and spring of character.

Men rob municipalities, pillage coffers, scandalize civilization and blacken the pages of history because they have hard, cold selfish hearts. Before a Christian becomes a tight-lipped, buttoned-up, boxed-in, closed-handed soldier, dying of spiritual suffocation, there is something wrong with the heart.

The kept heart is a warm heart, a burning heart that glows with fervent love toward the Lord, as He is revealed through the Word.

> Then he said unto them, O fools, and slow of heart to believe all that the prophets have spoken: ought not Christ to have suffered these things, and to enter into his glory? And beginning at Moses and all the prophets, he expounded unto them in all the scriptures the things concerning himself. . .And he said unto them, These are the words which I spake unto you, while I was yet with you, that all things must be fulfilled, which were written in the law of Moses, and in the prophets, and in the psalms, concerning me. Then opened he their understanding, that they might understand the scriptures (Luke 24:25-27, 44-45).

How sad when men and women have cold hearts, and sustain all relationships of life, discharging all duties, without the heavenly fire of deep and tender affection. The kept heart is a tender heart. How tragic when within men's bosoms beat hearts that are dead and miserable and insensible hearts that remind you of a tombstone, only not so white. The kept heart is a large heart. When we have largeness of heart, we can say: "The love of God hath been shed abroad in our hearts."

To make sure of this largeness of heart, we will not let sin reign in the heart, for sin contracts the heart, withers and blights it.

To make sure of this largeness of heart, we will eschew the vanity and pleasure of the world which always narrows the affections and loyalties of the heart.

And, of course, we know that selfishness — the insanity of existence, the abnormality of life — shrinks life to the narrow dimensions of the miniature and sends men out in pursuit of personal advantage, "elbowing others aside as they push their way to the front, making men wolves to other men." The selfish heart never treasures truth: "And this commandment we have from him, That he who loveth God love his brother also" (I John 4:21).

Wise was Watkinson who wrote: "We cannot walk with Christ, and have small hearts. The heart of our Lord was as big as the world, and broke for its redemption; and it is impossible to live in fellowship with Him without acquiring a proportionate magnanimity. We cannot walk with Christ, and have cold hearts. Our whole duty will then be performed not only with frigid conscientiousness but in the power and delight of a throbbing, bounding, constraining love. We cannot walk with Christ, and have hard hearts. The love of God, so wonderfully kind, will fill us with tender sympathy and melting pity. The school of the heart is the school of Christ; its great lesson-book, the New Testament; its grand symbol, the cross."

Now let us think upon the truth that

God's Eyes Are Upon the Heart

But the Lord said unto Samuel, Look not on his countenance, or on the height of his stature; because I have refused him: for the Lord seeth not as man seeth; for man looketh on the outward appearance, but the Lord looketh on the heart (I Sam. 16:7).

Blessed are the undefiled in the way, who walk in the law of the Lord. Blessed are they that keep his testimonies, and that seek him with the whole heart. They also do no iniquity: they walk in his ways. Thou hast commanded us to keep thy precepts diligently. O that my ways were directed to keep thy statutes! Then shall I not be ashamed, when I have respect unto all thy commandments (Ps. 119:1-6).

This Psalm shows how God understands the heart — the intellect, the thoughts, the reasonings, the will, the conscience.

Mr. Moody used to say: "Suppose a man should advertise
to take photographs of the heart — would he get many
customers?" And if our hearts had glass walls, would we want
curtains drawn over them? The Pharisees outwardly appeared
beautiful, but they received the severest censure and condemnation that Jesus ever gave. "They say, and do not" (Matt.
23:3). They were dogs in the manger.

> But woe unto you, scribes and Pharisees, hypocrites! for ye
> shut up the kingdom of heaven against men: for ye neither go in
> yourselves, neither suffer ye them that are entering to go in
> (Matt. 23:13).

They seized the property of widows.

> Woe unto you, scribes and Pharisees, hypocrities! for ye devour
> widow's houses, and for a pretence make long prayer; therefore ye
> shall receive the greater damnation (Matt 23:14).

They made proselytes to their ritualistic sham.

> Woe unto you, scribes, Pharisees, hypocrites! for ye compass
> sea and land to make one proselyte, and when he is made, ye
> make him twofold more the child of hell than yourselves (Matt.
> 23:15).

They were clean on the outside.

> Woe unto you, scribes and Pharisees, hypocrites! for ye
> make clean the outside of the cup and of the platter, but within
> they are full of extortion and excess. Thou blind Pharisee,
> cleanse first that which is within the cup and platter, that the
> outside of them may be clean also. Woe unto you, scribes and
> Pharisees, hypocrites! for ye are like unto whited sepulchres,
> which indeed appear beautiful outward, but are within full of
> dead men's bones, and of all uncleanness. Even so ye also out-
> wardly appear righteous unto men, but within ye are full of
> hypocrisy and iniquity (Matt. 23:25-28)

They were experts in adorning tombs with after-death tributes.

> Woe unto you, scribes and Pharisees, hypocrites! because ye
> build the tombs of the prophets, and garnish the sepulchres of
> the righteous, and say, If we had been in the days of our
> fathers we would not have been partakers with them in the

blood of the prophets. Wherefore ye be witnesses unto your-selves, that ye are the children of them which killed the prophets. Fill ye up then the measure of your fathers. Ye serpents, ye generation of vipers, how can ye escape the damnation of hell? (Matt. 23: 29-33).

"The Lord looketh on the heart" (I Sam. 16:7). He looked on Cain's heart when He said: "Where is Abel thy brother?" He looked on Elijah's heart when He said: "What doest thou here, Elijah?" He looked on Thomas' heart when He said: "Reach hither thy finger, and behold my hands." He looked on Philip's heart when He said, "Have I been so long time with you, and yet hast thou not known me, Philip?" He looked on Peter's heart when He said, "Simon, son of Jonas, lovest thou me more than these?" He looked on Saul's heart when on the Damascus road He said: "Saul, Saul, why persecutest thou me?"

The Bible is simply full of evidence of God's concern for the inward appearance, and the world is reeking with unholy evidence that man looketh on the outward appearance. Is God right, or is the world right?

Believers, and especially those in definite service for Christ, should neither deceive nor be deceived by appearance. The minister who preaches to a fashionable congregation should not use honeyed words of flattery out of a hypocritical heart to soothe the guilty consciences behind diamond studs and shimmering silk. The hypocrite in the pulpit is even a bigger sinner than the one in the pew! Hell fire is just as appropriate a subject for and up-and-out as for the down-and-out. Certainly the Master thought so.

And God, whose eyes are upon the heart, asks for the heart. He says: "Give me thine heart." God asks for the heart because He knows that mere culture will not change it. He knows that there must be an impartation of the divine nature. In the new birth, in the radical change of the heart whereby and wherein we become new creatures in Christ

Jesus, God yokes His holy nature with our fallen, helpless nature. God asks for the heart, because the only safe way of life for us is to yield our heart with all its wonderful power of affection and emotion and energy to divine control.

God says: "Keep *thy* heart." But He also says: "Give *Me* thy heart." It seems a strange way to keep the heart by giving it away. But history teaches there is such a thing as keeping by giving away. Napoleon left Egypt and went to the eastern shore of the Mediterranean with his army. He took Joppa as he passed and was about to take Acre also. The turks knew they could not hold Acre alone. They signaled to the British fleet for help. English stores and men came quickly. Turkey gave it to England in time of peril, and got it back when the danger was past.

The Fiji Islands are in the southern seas. This small group has 100,000 inhabitants, but is a wonderfully rich and productive territory. Some years ago their leading men looked out upon the world and felt they were in danger of losing their freedom. They saw France, Germany, Holland seizing all the territory they could find. Their turn would come next. They thought of a plan. England gave her colonies liberty. So they wrote to Queen Victoria and asked her to take under her protection the Fiji Islands. In 1874 they came under the English flag. They gave themselves to England to retain their liberty, to be protected from tyrannical foes. The heart of man is never held by himself — either evil or God will reign there. Christ knows all about the human heart. None can cleanse it and rule it and sweeten it as He can.

And we should not forget as we think of the body and the heart thereof that some day the heart will be a

DEAD HEART

Death is abroad, stalking his way to the door of hut and palace. Death comes — sometimes with the swiftness of lightning, sometimes inch by inch through the slow erosion of disease. But death is busy— in the city, in the country, everywhere.

"Death is a black camel which kneels at the door of all." "Death hath so many doors to let out life." Sir Thomas Browne speaks of "the one thousand doors that lead to death."

Robert Burns wails: "Fell Death's untimely frost, that nipt my flowers so early." And Bryant in "Thanatopsis" says: "All that tread this globe are but a handful to the tribes that slumber in its bosom." Gay in "Fables" says:

> The prince who kept the world in awe,
> The judge whose dictate fixed the law,
> The rich, the poor, the great, the small,
> Are levelled. Death confounds them all.

Bishop Hall said:

> Death Borders upon our birth,
> And our cradle stands in our grave.

Bishop Heber writes:

> Death rides on every passing breeze,
> He lurks in every flower.

Mrs. Hemans writes:

> Leaves have their time to fall,
> And flowers to wither at the north winds breath,
> And stars to set—but all
> Thou hast all seasons for thine own, O Death.

Pope wrote:

> Out — out are the lights — out all!
> And, over each quivering form,
> The curtain, a funeral pall,
> Comes down with the rush of a storm,
> And the angels, all pallid and wan,
> Uprising, unveiling, affirm
> That the play is the tragedy 'Man',
> And its hero the Conqueror, Worm.

All these are but saying in different words that the heart of the body will one day be a still heart. And then the eyes will see no more, the feet will walk no more, the ears will hear no more, the hands will work no more, the knees will bend no more, the mouth will speak no more.

Since this is true, let us say to God: "Thy word have I hid in my *heart* that I might not sin against thee." Let us make real these words of Paul:

> That Christ may dwell in your hearts by faith; that ye, being rooted and grounded in love, may be able to comprehend with all saints what is the breadth, and length, and depth, and height; and to know the love of Christ, which passeth knowledge, that ye might be filled with all the fulness of God (Eph. 3:17-19).

Remembering that the darkest spot on earth is a grave, let us have the cleaving heart (Acts 11:23). A heart that cleaves to the Lord is a heart that maintains unshaken faith and full confidence in the Lord's person and work. Such a heart will never accept any belittling statement concerning Christ's deity, will never admit any compromise in respect to His redeeming work, will always be closed against every form of error in respect to the person and work of Christ, whether it be destructive criticism or legalism. Such a heart will be utterly devoted to Jesus Christ.

Since of all the darkened glasses which mock us, the tombstone is the most opaque, since death is preluded by pain and terror, since its presence is accompanied by the agonies of separation — let us have the open heart, which is a believing heart. And a believing heart is a purified heart — flooded with the love of God.

> For this is the covenant I will make with the house of Israel after those days, saith the Lord; I will put my laws into their mind, and write them in their hearts: and I will be to them a God, and they shall be to me a people (Heb. 8:10).

> And a certain woman named Lydia, a seller of purple, of the city of Thyatira, which worshiped God, heard us: whose heart the Lord opened, that she attended unto the things which were spoken of Paul (Acts 16:14).

Since death is the strangest and bitterest of all enigmas, let us rejoice — as we give God our hearts, as we yield them to Him as instruments of righteousness — that there is the

DESTROYER OF DEATH

"The last enemy that shall be destroyed is death" (I Cor. 15:26). "Jesus Christ, who hath abolished death, and hath brought life and immortality to light through the gospel" (II Tim. 1:10).

That shows that Jesus Christ hath entered the arena. He who is Son of man without sin and Son of God with power has championed our cause. Singlehandedly against the malignant horde of hell, He fronts them in man's behalf — and "puts all enemies under his feet." Before the majestic aspect of His brow and beneath the uplifting of His mighty hand they fall. But is it, for Him, mere child's play? Nay. But it is a fierce and bloody conflict. Did not Christ at the outset, and for a moment, Himself go down covered with blood? Was not His visage more marred than any man's — and His countenance more than the sons of men? But, mustering the resources of the Godhead, did He not come up again to the dread encounter? And has not this strong enemy, death, for nearly two thousand years kept the field against the Son of God? Does not this enemy, entrenched in the depravities of the human heart, sheltered under the ramparts of the perverse human will, maintain a desperate defense against the advancing Conqueror?

But shall not "all enemies" — that old serpent, the Devil, and death, and hell, and sin — be put under Christ? Shall they not be cast down into the lake of fire? Shall not the time come, the blessed time, when "there shall be no more death"? Yes. The destruction of death will be the achievement of Jesus Christ. "The redemption of the body" is the last factor in the redemption and recovery of redeemed men from all the consequences of the fall. When the grasp of death upon their flesh is broken, the last vestige of the unhappy consequences of sin, so far as they are concerned, will disappear.

Yes, for them who believe on His name, death will be forever dead. Death's overthrow will be the last stroke of the great Champion and omnipotent Deliverer — the last triumphant blow in behalf of those oppressed by the darkness and terror thereof.

Then the chains of death will fall off.

Then will the prisoners of the grave go free.

Then the cry of a child at the couch of the dying mother will be heard no more.

Then the wail of the wife gazing upon her dead husband and her orphaned children shall rend the air no more.

Then the heartbroken husband, robbed of the wife of his bosom, will never be heard.

Then the tears will be wiped away from the faces of the sorrowing.

Then shall there be no more crying, nor sorrow, nor any pain, because "the former things are passed away."

Then the saved of the Lord shall "enter in through the gates into the city" and "have right to the tree of life." Then shall man be again in the garden of delights, with no flaming sword point thrusting him back from the tree. The crowned Conqueror of death gives His people a crown of life. Victorious over death through Him, they reign throughout all the ceaseless ages, "while the years of eternity roll."

Therefore, in the light of this truth, I beg you to be of "a willing heart toward God," "to serve Him with all your heart," to "do his commandments with all your heart," to remember that "the Lord is nigh to them that are of a broken heart," to "praise the Lord with all your heart," to have "the understanding that seeketh knowledge," to have "the heart that is right with God," to "purpose in your heart not to defile yourselves," to have "the heart that believeth unto righteousness," to have "gladness of heart, as when one goeth with a pipe to come to the mountain of the Lord, to the mighty One of Israel," to say now to God:

> Search me, O God, and know my heart: try me, and know my thoughts: and see if there be any wicked way in me, and lead me in the way everlasting (Ps. 139:23-24).

Chapter Ten

THE RESURRECTION BODY

*But some man will say, How are the dead raised up? and
with what body do they come?* (I Cor. 15:35).

Jesus was the "firstfruits" of the resurrection, the first sheaf
of the resurrection harvest. Does this mean He was the first
person who had been raised to life from the dead? Of course
not. Jesus had Himself raised Lazarus. Jesus had also given
the pallbearers in a funeral procession a holiday by calling to
life the dead son of the widow of Nain as he was being
carried to the grave. He also "astonished with a great astonishment" the folks in the home of Jairus when He caused to
bloom with life and strength and beauty the little flower cut
down by Death's keen scythe (Mark 5:42). And many years
before this Elisha had raised to life the dead son of the Shuna-
mite woman. But these risings from the dead were not resur-
rections as was the resurrection of Jesus — and will be that
of every follower of Jesus in the time of resurrection. Jesus'
natural body had been changed to a spiritual body. His
mortal body had put on immortality. That which was sown
in humiliation had been raised in glory. So shall all the redeemed be changed in the resurrection.

There are also celestial bodies, and bodies terrestrial: but
the glory of the celestial is one, and the glory of the terrestrial
is another. There is one glory of the sun, and another glory
of the moon, and another glory of the stars: for one star differeth
from another star in glory. So also is the resurrection of the
dead. It is sown in corruption; it is raised in incorruption: it

is sown in dishonour; it is raised in glory: it is sown in weakness; it is raised in power: It is sown a natural body; it is raised a spiritual body. There is a natural body, and there is a spiritual body (I Cor. 15:40-44).

Thus we see something of the nature of the resurrection body. Being different from the body that now is in that it will be freed from the limitations to which our earthly bodies are subject, yet the resurrection body will have a real identity to the earthly body. Thus do we have assurance of the permanence of personality and individuality. And this new body will be a wonderfully habitable instrument for the soul under the new conditions of the eternal world. And in the eternal world, I shall remain I and you will remain you. Thus God guarantees to us the comfort of recognition and assures us that heaven is not the abiding place of viewless and disembodied spirits, but a place where everyone has his body.

By the truth and love of God, we can rest assured that the resurrection body will be a body — not something vague, misty, intangible. Though the resurrection body will be a spiritual body — a body designed for the life of the Spirit, a body subject to spiritual rather than to natural laws — it will be a real body, no ghostlike body, but a body, as real as that of the Lord Jesus who could be seen, could be handled, could share food with others. And the resurrection body will be a body that can occupy space, and yet pass through natural obstacles such as doors or walls or space without the slightest difficulty. And the resurrection body of every Christian will be immortal — never subject to the touch of death. Forever will it be free from any possibility of sin, of disease, of death, being a replica of the glorified body of the Lord Jesus.

> Beloved, now are we the sons of God, and it doth not yet appear what we shall be: but we know that, when he shall appear, we shall be like him, for we shall see him as he is (I John 3:2).

There will be none of the taint of Adam's fall in the resurrection body. The eradication of the carnal nature, so fondly claimed by some today, will then be a reality for every child of God.

In the resurrection body there will be no sickness, no growing old, no infirmity.

> Because the creature itself also shall be delivered from the bondage of corruption into the glorious liberty of the children of God (Rom. 8:21).

In the Bible, we find these words:

> And not only they, but ourselves also, which have the first-fruits of the Spirit, even we ourselves groan within ourselves, waiting for the adoption, to wit, the redemption of our body (Rom. 8:23).

So the resurrection body is a redeemed body — redeemed from sin itself, from the results of sin, from the death of sin, as well as the tendency and bent to sin. Nor will weariness ever beset the glorious and incorruptible resurrection body.

Dr. Wilbur Smith writes: "The characteristics of our resurrection life and our resurrection bodies are in strongest contrast to what we see around us. With the dissolutions of governments and cities, and laws, and the death of so many, we can thank God for the day when we shall live in incorruptible bodies. In contrast to the shame and injustice of today is the glory of the life that is yet to come. In contrast to the comparative weakness of the righteous followers of Christ today against the monstrous forces of evil and Antichrist is the assurance finally of superior and permanent power. Against the naturalism, humanism and materialism of the world we have the spirituality of that life presented to us, and in contrast with the earthliness of so much that we here experience is the assurance of the heavenliness of the life that we have in Christ."

> And as we have borne the image of the earthy, we shall also bear the image of the heavenly (I Cor. 15:49).

The "image of the heavenly" is Jesus. He is "the first begotten of the dead" (Rev. 1:5). He is the "firstfruit," of which believers are the after fruit. He is our pattern. God assures us that if and when our "earthly house of this tabernacle were dissolved, we have a building of God, a house not made with hands eternal in the heavens" (II Cor. 5:1).

Dr. John W. Bradbury writes: "The resurrection of the believer's body is involved in the deepest expectations of the enlightened heart. The whole creation travails for this eventful hour. With the final breaking of the bondage of death there will be the smash-up of the 'bondage of corruption' which enmeshes this world. 'Creation groaneth and travaileth in pain together until now.' Because the light of God has shined in our hearts, we also 'groan' under the burden of this world's need. But we also know that the time for the release of creation's bonds coincides with 'the redemption of our body'" (Rom. 8:19-24).

> For our conversation is in heaven; from whence also we look for the Saviour, the Lord Jesus Christ: who shall change our vile body, that it may be fashioned like unto his glorious body, according to the working whereby he is able even to subdue all things unto himself (Phil. 3:20-21).

Do we not, then, think Scripturally when we say that the resurrection body will be like the resurrection body of Jesus? Will not the resurrection body be a literal and physical body with flesh and bones like the disciples felt when they put their hands upon the resurrected Jesus?

> Behold my hands and my feet, that it is I myself: handle me, and see; for the spirit hath not flesh and bones, as ye see me have. . . .And they gave him a piece of a broiled fish, and of an honeycomb. And he took it, and did eat before them" (Luke 24:39-43).

One noted preacher wrote: "At the last supper, Jesus ate and drank with the disciples and said, 'But I say unto you, I will not drink henceforth of this fruit of the vine, until that day when I drink it new with you in my Father's kingdom'

(Matt. 26:29). So in the heavenly kingdom Christians will eat and drink with Jesus Christ. And no doubt the fruit of the tree of life is literal fruit, and these resurrected and glorified bodies will be, like the perfect bodies of Adam and Eve in the Garden of Eden, sustained by food and drink, in perfect health. And that indicates, I think, that there will be fluids in the bodies, and so blood as well as flesh and bones."

Dr. W. E. Denham, great and good Bible teacher for years, writes: "The resurrection body will be like that of the Lord Jesus. That body had several characteristics. First, it was in appearance like His earthly body, since the disciples recognized Him. Second it differed from His earthly body, since Mary, and the two on the Emmaus Road did not at first recognize Him. Perhaps the resurrection body will be similar to that which we possess now but will have the power to change its appearance whenever desired. Third, it will be a physical body. Our Lord was able to eat with His disciples. He challenged them to handle Him. Such things could not have been possible had He not possessed a physical body. Fourth, this physical body will be animated by spiritual and not by mortal life. Fifth, it will have certain glorious qualities not possessed by us now. It will be deathless and, so far as we can see, not subject to any form of sickness or weakness or weariness. It will be free from limitations of time and space. Our Lord could appear in a closed room. It will possess unlimited possibilities. Sixth, it will be perfect. By this I do not mean that twisted limbs will be made straight. I do not know about that. I have sometimes thought that heaven's standards of beauty may be so different from earth's that what we call deformity here may be beauty there. Certain I am that the spiritual beauties will be the important ones."

Dr. Walter L. Wilson says: "Just as the little grain of popcorn is planted in the soil and produces a stalk on which are many grains of little popcorn; just as the acorn is planted and from that tiny grave there emerges that which produces similar acorns: so will the body that is planted be raised in its own likeness for like produces like. The 'it' that is buried as described in I Corinthians 15:43 is the same 'it' that is raised from that grave.

"A story is told concerning Michael Faraday, the great chemist. It is said that a lady sent him a gold cup to be tested for its gold content. The cup was accidently dropped into a cask of chemically pure acid and was soon dissolved. Not a trace of the cup could be seen, there was only the clear, amber colored liquid in the vessel. Mr. Faraday called for a proper reagent which he stirred into the acid and soon a gold precipitate began falling to the bottom of the cask. After he thought all the gold had settled, he poured off the acid, washed the powder and sent it to the goldsmith who had originally made the cup. He told him of his predicament. The goldsmith found the original pattern of the cup, melted the gold powder, poured it into the mold and soon reproduced the cup. He returned it to Mr. Faraday who made the necessary tests and then sent the cup back to the owner with his report.

"Mr. Faraday made a cup from the grave of the cup where there was no cup. The cup had been dissolved and the particles were scattered throughout the acid. The cup was a new one although made of the old materials and was exactly like the original.

"So our wonderful Lord, the Creator, will, in the resurrection, make a duplicate body exactly like the one that was buried. The body that has been used for the glory of God, the service of Christ, and the blessing of men, will be raised to be rewarded. The body that has been used to serve Satan and to promote his cause will be raised to be punished. With the body, we do well or do evil; therefore, the body will be blessed or punished after the resurrection."

Dr. E. Schuyler English writes: "Our present bodies are

terrestrial and are subject to natural laws. Our resurrection bodies will be celestial, subject to a different set of laws. The resurrection body will be like the body that our Lord Jesus Christ had upon His resurrection, for He is 'the firstfruits' of all those who die in faith. His body was a body of flesh and bones (Luke 24:39). The celestial body will be a spiritual body, a body of glory, a body of power. His resurrection body, His body of glory, a glory which He will share with His own (John 17:22), was not limited by space or matter (John 20:19), and so we assume that our resurrection bodies will enjoy like freedom from the laws that we know today."

Dr. Gaines S. Dobbins of the Southern Baptist Theological Seminary, writes: "This quality of everlastingness belongs to every soul, whether saved or unsaved. The spiritual body given to the Christian's soul will be like unto that which Christ possessed when he was raised from the dead. It will be real, recognizable, identifiable, but incorruptible. We who are given this redeemed and imperishable body will be like Christ, for we shall see Him as He is. That we should have a spiritual and immortal body is no more incredible than that we should now have a marvelous, although mortal, body, one the soul's temporal dwelling-place, the other its eternal abode. Truly the mystery is great, but not contrary to experience and reason."

Dr. Duke K. McCall, now president of the Southern Baptist Theological Seminary, writes: "No matter what the resurrection body is like, it will be better. It will be a spiritual body and not a natural body. It will be an incorruptible body and not a corruptible one. There will, however, be a continuity. It will be my body. It seemed that I could hear friends in glory gasp in astonishment at the moment of recognition and then exclaim, 'What a marvelous improvement; I hardly knew you!' But of course, they will know me because it will be my body sown in mortality but raised in immortality. I thought how wonderful it would be to have a body freed from the limitations of time and space, from sin and suffering, from sickness and death. The problem of explaining such a body occurred to me, but I find it no more difficult to accept the idea than it is to accept the new space-time conception of higher mathematics. Einstein's new unified field theory is much more of a puzzle than how this resurrected body may be provided. Why? The answer is because the Lord of life abundant and eternal will provide it out of the matchless glory of His love."

Dr. Fred W. Kendall, pastor of the First Baptist Church, Jackson, Tennessee, writes: "God's creative power will reach a climax beyond the present knowledge or imagination of man in the glorified lives of resurrected men. The complete goal of creation and spiritual redemption will be realized. The heavenly bodies will be in supreme contrast to the earthly ones. Earthly bodies were victims of the curse of sin. They were mortal, doomed to wither and die, subject to disease, suffering and pain. Resurrected bodies will be free from the curse of sin, and therefore will be free from all pain and death. Earthly bodies were instruments of sin and temptation, and the flesh was an enemy of spiritual perfection and growth. The resurrected bodies will be agents of spiritual growth, freed from sin's attacks, aiding spiritual growth and attainments. Earthly bodies were physical, adapted to a physical environment, serving as a medium between man and the physical world. The resurrection body will be spiritual and will serve as a medium of man's fellowship with God in a heavenly environment. The earthly body was like that of the first Adam and was of the animal order. The resurrected body will be like Christ, the second Adam, freed from all animal appetites and passions. There will be marks of identity between the earthly and resurrected bodies. We shall know each other, and we shall know as we are known."

Dr. J. Wash Watts wrote: "His resurrected body bore

evidence of earthy experiences, and He used that evidence to show that the 'I' of the cross was the same 'I' revealed by the nail-scarred hands. 'Then were the disciples glad, when they saw the Lord' (John 20:20). The identity of the resurrected Jesus with the human Jesus changed the evidence of death to evidence of life, the evidence of shame to evidence of glory, the evidence of weakness to evidence of power."

This corruptible must put on incorruption (I Cor. 15:53).

I recall a beautiful passage from the pen of Dr. W. B. Riley: "It is the one note of joy for the bereaved. Nothing that has ever come into the world has so scarred its face, and so sorrow-ed human hearts as the spade of the cemetery sexton. The author often drives through beautiful Lakewood. In spring-time, all nature breaks into beauty there. The blooming flowers are as fresh and fragrant as the season; the green sward is a landscape of God indeed; the monuments and obelisks are expressions of classic beauty, marking the resting places of the beloved dead. But he hates the cemetery, none the less! It has started too many tears, broken too many hearts, destroyed too many homes, dissipated too much happiness, given rise to too great sorrow and grief; it has shown too little pity for bereaved mothers; too little concern for broken-hearted fathers; too slight a sorrow for suffering brothers and sisters. The only way that one can be happy, and yet wander in the realm where the last enemy has conquered, is to keep in mind the promise of resurrection, and anticipate the day when the provisions of this text shall be perfected and the graves of the believers shall be broken up; the day when the beauty of the trees, the fragrance of the flowers and the music of the birds shall be exceeded a hundredfold, yea, a thousand, by the hosts of God's redeemed, standing in triumph over the last Enemy, clad 'in white,' having conquered corruption."

Therein is the promise of redemption from the grave. Our bodies that shall be — all corruption gone, all mortality gone, all weakness gone, all dishonor removed, all carnal appetites destroyed. A woeful sense of inadequacy oppresses when one attempts to imagine the glory and beauty of such a body. But take heed to these words:

> "The Saviour, the Lord Jesus Christ. . .shall change our vile body, that it may be fashioned like unto his glorious body, according to the working whereby he is able even to subdue all things unto himself" (Phil. 3:21).

God answers all questions about the new bodies of the redeemed by showing that the future body of the believer will be like the body that the Lord Jesus had when He was raised from the dead. (Phil. 3:20-21).

Dr. Donald Grey Barnhouse, in a beautiful passage in his book *Guaranteed Deposits,* says: "Jesus Christ had a body that was subject to the frailties of our race. He became hungry, tired, sleepy. He was arrested, tried and nailed to a cross. From the wounds there flowed His blood. He died. His body was put into a tomb. A great stone was rolled in front of the tomb. Three days later there came angels from heaven who rolled away the stone from the door. He was not there. It is evident that His resurrection body was subject to natural laws that are, as yet, undiscovered. He had come through the material stone and was not in the tomb. A few days later, when the disciples were in an upper room with the doors shut, He appeared in the midst of them. Again it was seen that the laws which govern these bodies of ours did not govern the body in which he was raised from the dead. Yet it was a material, tangible body. He told the doubting Thomas not to be faithless but to believe. 'Behold my hands and my feet, that it is I myself,' He said; 'handle me, and see; for a spirit hath not flesh and bones, as ye see me have' (Luke 24:39).

"Once more He demonstrated that His resurrection body was not subject to the ordinary physical limitations, for while they gazed upon Him, He was taken up from them into heaven, and a cloud received Him out of their sight.

"When we are told that we are to have bodies like unto His glorified body, we know that we are to have bodies like this one that He had at His resurrection. It was the same body — make no mistake about that — it was the same body in which He died; but it was changed, transformed body — a body of glory. Ours shall be like His. Take courage, you who are blind, and you who lie on invalid couches. Take courage, you who go down into old age. Take courage, you who have lost a dear one to death. We shall be like Christ."

"How are the dead raised up?" By the power of God. This is the promise of the Almighty. Did not God create man out of dust in His own image? Did God not breathe into man the breath of life? Did not man then become a living soul? Then cannot God raise the dead body and give it back to the soul which has never died?

> But if the Spirit of him that raised up Jesus from the dead dwell in you, he that raised up Christ from the dead shall also quicken your mortal bodies by his Spirit that dwelleth in you (Rom 8:11).
>
> And God hath both raised up the Lord, and will also raise up us by his own power (I Cor. 6:14).

In this *actual* resurrection, what was buried shall rise again. What went into the tomb shall come out of the tomb. Personal identity shall be perfectly preserved in the resurrection process. The Bible asserts the sureness of the resurrection body.

Paul likens the resurrection to the sowing and sprouting of a grain of wheat. A grain of wheat always produces itself whenever it sprouts. Dr. J. L. White says, speaking of this: "There are imitations — the tare, but a tare is never wheat. We cannot tell just how a spear of golden grain will look next June, but we do know it will be the same individual wheat plant. So we do know from the perfections of the analogy, when we bury the body, that the same identical man shall rise on the resurrection morn. Identity shall be absolutely preserved. And we

know that translation of Enoch is divine testimony that the
body itself is capable of eternal life."

In the resurrection of believers their bodies shall be transformed and fashioned like "the body of his glory." We catch
a glimpse of that glory in the transfiguration of Jesus where
and when the spiritual incandesence of His deity burst out
from the prison house of His flesh and made His face to
shine like the sun and His garments to be whiter than luminous snow (Matt. 17:2). Concerning this resurrection change
in the body Dr. Gordon strikingly says: "The charcoal and the
diamond are the same substance — only the one is carbon in
its humiliation and the other carbon in its glory. So is the
tabernacle in which we dwell, in comparison with our house
which is from heaven. The one is mortal flesh shadowed by
the curse and doomed to be sown in dishonor; the other is
that flesh made immortal and marvelously transformed."

Grand will be the scene and sweet the joy of the first resurrection — when the trumpet shall sound and the graves shall
open and the sea shall give up the bodies of all believers.
Weeping mother, sad father, broken-hearted wife, thy dead
believing one shall rise again. You who live in the house
where the little chair is empty and the prattling voice of the
lovely baby has been hushed in death, your dead you shall
have again. You broken-hearted, think upon the promises of
Christ — and wipe away your tears; for you shall meet your
believing dead again. Walk, all you Christians, out into the
cemetery where the gloom of death has settled — and drive
away your darkness with the light of this glorious truth and
hope.

Let us, faithful unto Christ in all things and in all places,
rejoice in that some blessed day, with all our fightings done,
our bodies shall be conformed to the body of His glory (Phil.
3:21) — a spiritual body adapted to the spiritual existence
into which entrance is gained by the resurrection. Let us

rejoice in that God has supremely honored the human body by the incarnation of His holy Son — and God has greatly honored His servants to be like Him and with Him in glory forever and forever.